PRENTICE HALL

WORLD STUDIES
THE ANCIENT WORLD

Reading and Vocabulary Study Guide

Boston, Massachusetts
Upper Saddle River, New Jersey

The map on page 88 is based on a map created by DK Cartography.

ISBN 0-13-204229-0

13 14 15 16 17 V0UD 18 17 16 15 14

Table of Contents

Chapter 5 Ancient China

Chapter 6 Ancient Greece

Chapter 7 Ancient Rome

How to Use This Book

The Reading and Vocabulary Study Guide was designed to help you understand World Studies content. It will also help you build your reading and vocabulary skills. Please take the time to look at the next few pages to see how it works!

The Prepare to Read page gets you ready to read each section.

Objectives from your textbook help you focus your reading.

With each chapter, you will study a Target Reading Skill. This skill is introduced in your textbook, but explained more here. Later, questions or activities in the margin will help you practice the skill.

You are given a new Vocabulary Strategy with each chapter. Questions or activities in the margin later will help you practice the strategy.

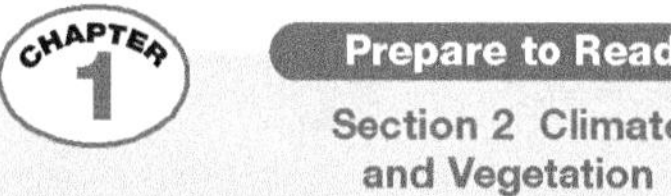

Prepare to Read

Section 2 Climate and Vegetation

Objectives

1. Find out what kinds of climate Latin America has.
2. Learn what factors influence climate in Latin America.
3. Understand how climate and vegetation influence the ways people live.

Target Reading Skill

Preview and Predict Before you read, make a prediction or a guess about what you will be learning. Predicting is another way to set a purpose for reading. It will help you remember what you read. Follow these steps: (1) Preview the section title, objectives, headings, and table on the pages in Section 2. (2) Predict something you might learn about Latin America. Based on your preview, you will probably predict that you will learn more about Latin America's climate and plants.

List two facts that you predict you will learn about Latin America's climate and plants.

____

____

As you read, check your predictions. How correct were they? If they were not very accurate, try to pay closer attention when you preview.

Vocabulary Strategy

Using Context Clues to Determine Meaning You will probably come across words you haven't seen before when you read. Sometimes you can pick up clues about the meaning of an unfamiliar word by reading the words, phrases, and sentences that surround it. The underlined words in the sentences below give clues to the meaning of the word *dense*.

The Amazon rain forest is ***dense*** with plants and trees. The plant life is <u>so crowded</u> that almost <u>no sunlight reaches the ground</u>.

Unfamiliar Word	Clues	Meaning
dense	so crowded no sunlight	thick, close together crowded

Section Summary pages provide an easy-to-read summary of each section.

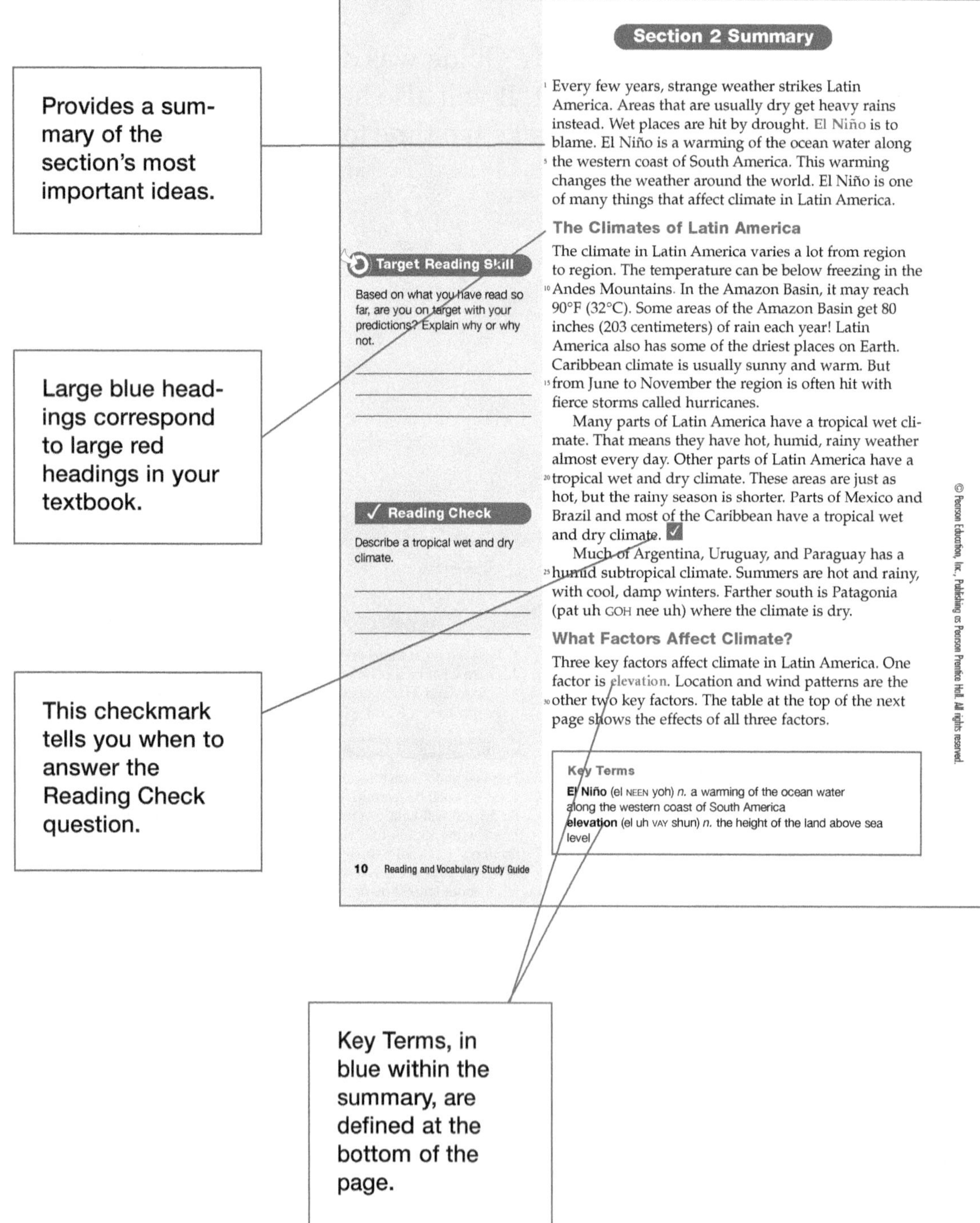

Section 2 Summary

Every few years, strange weather strikes Latin America. Areas that are usually dry get heavy rains instead. Wet places are hit by drought. El Niño is to blame. El Niño is a warming of the ocean water along the western coast of South America. This warming changes the weather around the world. El Niño is one of many things that affect climate in Latin America.

The Climates of Latin America

The climate in Latin America varies a lot from region to region. The temperature can be below freezing in the Andes Mountains. In the Amazon Basin, it may reach 90°F (32°C). Some areas of the Amazon Basin get 80 inches (203 centimeters) of rain each year! Latin America also has some of the driest places on Earth. Caribbean climate is usually sunny and warm. But from June to November the region is often hit with fierce storms called hurricanes.

Many parts of Latin America have a tropical wet climate. That means they have hot, humid, rainy weather almost every day. Other parts of Latin America have a tropical wet and dry climate. These areas are just as hot, but the rainy season is shorter. Parts of Mexico and Brazil and most of the Caribbean have a tropical wet and dry climate. ✓

Much of Argentina, Uruguay, and Paraguay has a humid subtropical climate. Summers are hot and rainy, with cool, damp winters. Farther south is Patagonia (pat uh GOH nee uh) where the climate is dry.

What Factors Affect Climate?

Three key factors affect climate in Latin America. One factor is elevation. Location and wind patterns are the other two key factors. The table at the top of the next page shows the effects of all three factors.

Target Reading Skill

Based on what you have read so far, are you on target with your predictions? Explain why or why not.

✓ Reading Check

Describe a tropical wet and dry climate.

Key Terms

El Niño (el NEEN yoh) *n.* a warming of the ocean water along the western coast of South America

elevation (el uh VAY shun) *n.* the height of the land above sea level

10 Reading and Vocabulary Study Guide

Questions and activities in the margin help you take notes on main ideas, and practice the Target Reading Skill and Vocabulary Strategy.

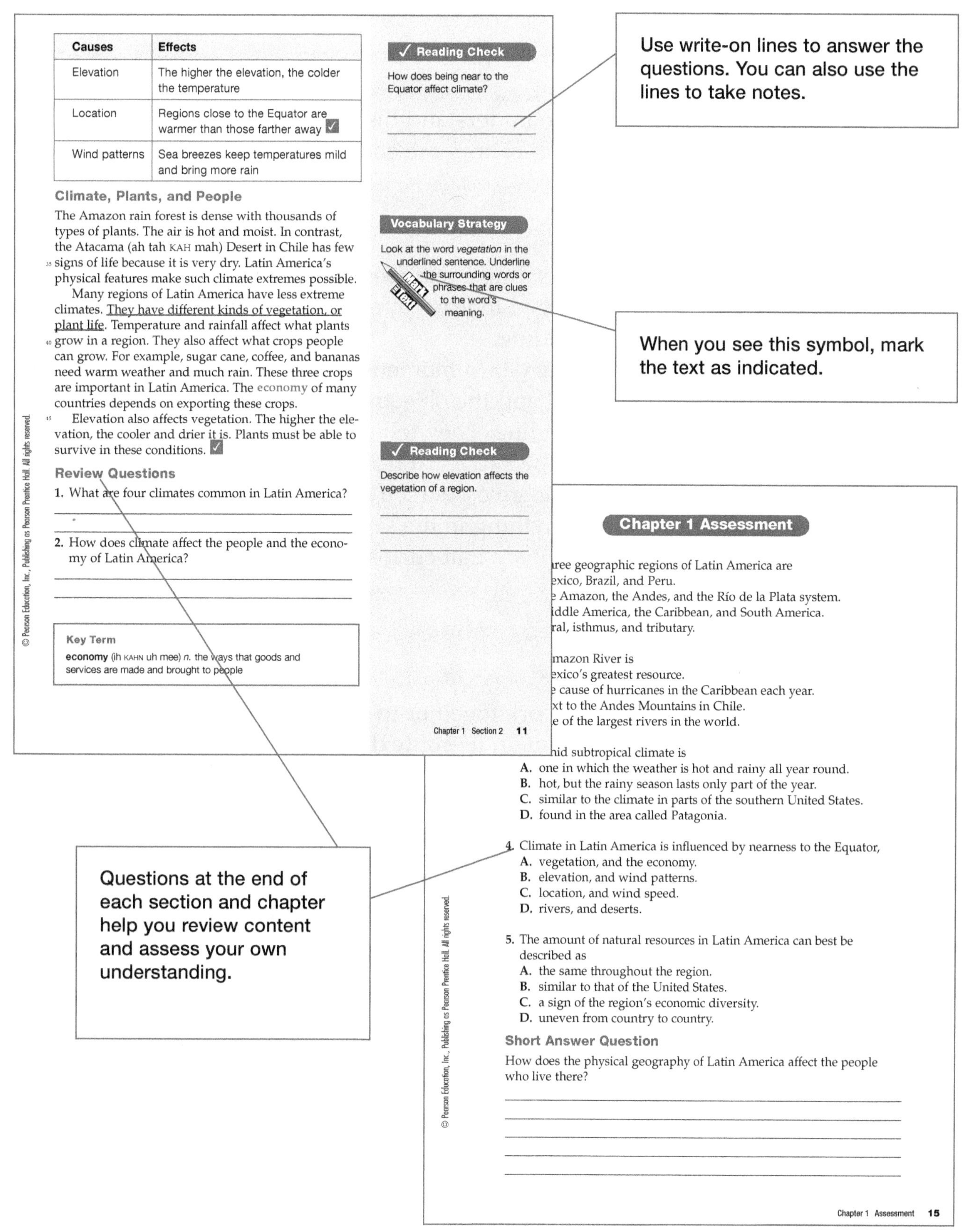

Causes	Effects
Elevation	The higher the elevation, the colder the temperature
Location	Regions close to the Equator are warmer than those farther away ☑
Wind patterns	Sea breezes keep temperatures mild and bring more rain

Climate, Plants, and People

The Amazon rain forest is dense with thousands of types of plants. The air is hot and moist. In contrast, the Atacama (ah tah KAH mah) Desert in Chile has few signs of life because it is very dry. Latin America's physical features make such climate extremes possible.

Many regions of Latin America have less extreme climates. They have different kinds of vegetation, or plant life. Temperature and rainfall affect what plants grow in a region. They also affect what crops people can grow. For example, sugar cane, coffee, and bananas need warm weather and much rain. These three crops are important in Latin America. The economy of many countries depends on exporting these crops.

Elevation also affects vegetation. The higher the elevation, the cooler and drier it is. Plants must be able to survive in these conditions. ☑

Review Questions

1. What are four climates common in Latin America?

2. How does climate affect the people and the economy of Latin America?

Key Term

economy (ih KAHN uh mee) *n.* the ways that goods and services are made and brought to people

✓ **Reading Check**

How does being near to the Equator affect climate?

Vocabulary Strategy

Look at the word *vegetation* in the underlined sentence. Underline the surrounding words or phrases that are clues to the word's meaning.

✓ **Reading Check**

Describe how elevation affects the vegetation of a region.

© Pearson Education, Inc., Publishing as Pearson Prentice Hall. All rights reserved.

Chapter 1 Section 2 **11**

Chapter 1 Assessment

...ree geographic regions of Latin America are
...exico, Brazil, and Peru.
...e Amazon, the Andes, and the Río de la Plata system.
...iddle America, the Caribbean, and South America.
...ral, isthmus, and tributary.

...mazon River is
...exico's greatest resource.
...e cause of hurricanes in the Caribbean each year.
...xt to the Andes Mountains in Chile.
...e of the largest rivers in the world.

...hid subtropical climate is
A. one in which the weather is hot and rainy all year round.
B. hot, but the rainy season lasts only part of the year.
C. similar to the climate in parts of the southern United States.
D. found in the area called Patagonia.

4. Climate in Latin America is influenced by nearness to the Equator,
A. vegetation, and the economy.
B. elevation, and wind patterns.
C. location, and wind speed.
D. rivers, and deserts.

5. The amount of natural resources in Latin America can best be described as
A. the same throughout the region.
B. similar to that of the United States.
C. a sign of the region's economic diversity.
D. uneven from country to country.

Short Answer Question

How does the physical geography of Latin America affect the people who live there?

© Pearson Education, Inc., Publishing as Pearson Prentice Hall. All rights reserved.

Chapter 1 Assessment **15**

Prepare to Read

Section 1
Geography and History

Objectives

1. Learn what tools are used to understand history.
2. Find out how geography and history are connected.

Target Reading Skill

Preview and Set a Purpose Reading a textbook is different from reading a novel or the newspaper. To read to learn effectively, you must preview and set a purpose for your reading.

Before you read this section, take a moment to preview it. Look at the title "Geography and History" and the objectives. Now flip through the next two pages. Read each heading. They tell you about the section's contents. They tell you what to expect to learn from each section. As you preview, use this information to give yourself a reason to read the section. Are you curious about anything in the section, like how people learn about history? Read to satisfy that curiosity—that's your purpose for reading.

Vocabulary Strategy

Using Context Clues Words work together to explain meaning. The meaning of a word may depend on its **context**. A word's context is the other words and sentences that surround it. The context gives you clues to a word's meaning.

Try this example. Say that you do not know the meaning of the word *history* in the following sentence:

> "History began when people started to keep written records of their experiences."

You could ask yourself: "What information does the sentence give me about the word?" Answer: "I know that history began when people started writing down their experiences. This tells me that history must be the written record of human experience."

Section 1 Summary

In 1991 two hikers found the frozen body of a man in the Alps. They called the frozen man the Iceman. Scientists studied his clothing, tools, and body. They hoped to learn about the Iceman's life and death. The scientists learned that he lived about 5,000 years ago. The most important clue was the Iceman's copper ax. Europeans first used copper in about 4000 B.C. The ax told scientists that the Iceman lived after people had learned to use copper.

Understanding History

Humans want to know what life was like long ago. About 5,000 years ago, people began writing down what happened to them. That was the beginning of **history**. The time before people learned to write is called **prehistory**.

To learn about life in prehistoric times, scientists can't study written records. They must use other kinds of clues. **Archaeologists** are scientists who study objects to learn about the past. Objects such as bones and tools tell them how people lived. For example, the size of a spear point can tell whether it was used to kill a large or small animal.

Historians don't just use objects to learn about the past. They also study written records. Many written records began as **oral traditions**. They were passed down by word of mouth. They tell stories about heroes or things that happened. Not all oral stories are accurate. People often mix facts with tall tales about heroes. Still, oral stories tell historians how people lived and what they thought was important. ✓

Key Terms

history (HIS tuh ree) *n.* the written events of people
prehistory (pree HIS tuh ree) *n.* time before writing was invented
archaeologist (ahr kee AHL u jist) *n.* a scientist who studies objects to learn about the past
oral traditions (AWR ul truh DISH unz) *n.* stories passed down by word of mouth

Target Reading Skill

If you want to learn about studying history, how does reading about archaeologists help you meet your goal?

____

____

____

✓ Reading Check

Why are historians interested in oral traditions?

____

____

____

Linking Geography and History

It is important to know when something happened. But historians want to know more. They want to understand *why* things happened. To do this, they often look at **geography**. Geography is the study of the earth's surface and how it was shaped. It also refers to a place's climate, landscape, and location.

Often geography and history are linked. Many things affect people's lives. Whether a place is hot or cold affects the lives of the people who live there. So does its water supply. For example, the geography of Egypt helps explain why the ancient Egyptians had a successful civilization.

Egyptian civilization was built on the banks of the Nile River in Africa. Each year, the Nile flooded. Rich soil was left on the river banks. Because of this, Egyptian farmers were able to grow large crops. They were able to feed large numbers of people in cities. That meant that not everyone had to farm. Some people could do other kinds of jobs. That helped develop the civilization. Without the Nile and its floods, Egyptian civilization would not have done so well. This is one way geography affects history. ✓

Vocabulary Strategy

What does the word *civilization* mean in the underlined sentence? What clues can you find in the surrounding words, phrases, or sentences? Circle the words in this paragraph that could help you learn what *civilization* means.

Mark the Text

✓ Reading Check

Give one example of geography's effect on history.

____

____

____

Review Questions

1. What do scientists study to learn about prehistory?

____

____

____

2. How can geography help us understand history?

____

____

____

Key Term

geography (jee AHG ruh fee) *n.* the study of Earth's surface and how it is shaped

Prepare to Read

Section 2 Prehistory

Objectives

1. Discover how hunter-gatherers lived during the Stone Age.
2. Learn about the beginning of farming.

Target Reading Skill

Preview and Predict Making predictions about what you will learn from your text helps you set a purpose for reading. It also helps you remember what you have read. Before you begin reading, preview the section. Look at the section title and objectives above, then the headings. Then predict what the section will tell you. Based on your preview, you will probably predict that this section will tell you about how early humans lived.

List two facts that you expect to learn about how early humans lived.

Prediction 1: ____

Prediction 2: ____

As you read, check your predictions. Were they right? If they were not very accurate, you may need to pay closer attention while you preview the section.

Vocabulary Strategy

Using Context Clues Sometimes you can pick up clues about an unfamiliar word's meaning from the words, phrases, and sentences around it. The underlined words in the paragraph below give clues to the meaning of the word *nomad*.

> Many of our Old Stone Age ancestors were **nomads**. They moved around to places where they thought they would find food. They stayed there for several days. When they had gathered all the food around them, they moved on.

A nomad is a person who travels from place to place instead of settling in one place. The underlined phrases told you that information.

Section 2 Summary

Stone Age Hunting and Gathering

The **Stone Age** was the earliest known period of human culture. **Hominids**, including early humans, began using stone to create tools. They also made tools from wood and animal bones. The Stone Age continued until people learned to use metal for tools.

Archaeologists divide the Stone Age into three periods: the Old Stone Age, the Middle Stone Age, and the New Stone Age. During the Old Stone Age, early hominids did not yet know how to farm. They lived by hunting animals and gathering wild plants. Over time they learned to hunt in groups. Most of human prehistory took place during the Old Stone Age.

Early hominids first learned to use fire between 1,400,000 and 500,000 years ago. Early hominids later learned to create fire. With fire to keep them warm, people could move to areas with cold climates.

As early hominids learned to use tools, they left their original homes in Africa. This may have occurred as early as one million years ago. Many early hominids were **nomads**. They moved around to places where they thought they would find food. When they had finished gathering all the food around them, they moved on. ✓

Early hominids eventually spread over much of Earth.

When	Event
At least 500,000 years ago	Early hominids are living in Asia and Europe
More than 100,000 years ago	Modern humans originated in Africa
About 30,000 years ago	Humans cross Asia to North America

Key Terms

Stone Age (stohn ayj) ***n.*** a period of time during which people made tools and weapons from stone

hominid (HAHM uh nid) ***n.*** a modern human or a member of an earlier group that may have included ancestors or relatives of modern humans

nomad (NOH mad) ***n.*** a person who has no settled home

Target Reading Skill

Based on what you have read so far, are your predictions on target? If not, change your predictions now.

New Predictions: ____________

____

____

____

✓ Reading Check

What was life like during the Stone Age?

____

____

____

The Beginning of Farming

People lived by hunting and gathering food for tens of thousands of years. During the Middle Stone Age, people learned to make better tools. About 11,000 years ago, people learned to grow their own food. This was the beginning of the New Stone Age. They no longer had to be nomads.

At the same time, some people became pastoral nomads. Pastoral nomads raised livestock. They traveled in search of grass for their animals. There are still pastoral nomads in some countries today.

In most societies, women were in charge of farming. Men were usually hunters.

Some places were better for farming than others. Soil in some areas was very fertile. In several places around the world, the soil, water, and length of growing seasons were good for plants. People there became farmers. Over time, people learned how to grow better, more useful plants.

During the New Stone Age, humans learned to **domesticate** animals. Dogs were used for hunting. Sheep, goats, and pigs gave meat, milk, wool, and skins. By about 2400 B.C., cattle, camels, horses, and donkeys were used to carry heavy loads. Domesticated animals helped people make sure they would have a steady supply of food. ✓

Vocabulary Strategy

Mark the Text

Look at the phrase *pastoral nomads* in the underlined sentence. The term is not defined for you. But there are clues to what it means. Write the definition below, then circle the words or phrases that helped you learn its meaning.

____

____

____

✓ Reading Check

What skills did people develop during the New Stone Age?

____

____

____

Review Questions

1. What important skills did early hominids of the Old Stone Age use to find food?

____

____

____

2. What marked the start of the New Stone Age?

____

____

____

Key Terms

domesticate (duh MES tih kayt) *v.* tame wild plants and animals for human use

Prepare to Read

Section 3 The Beginnings of Civilization

Objectives

1. Find out the advantages people gained from settling in one place.
2. Learn about the growth of early cities.
3. Understand how the first civilizations formed and spread.

Target Reading Skill

Preview and Ask Questions Before you read this section, preview the section title, objectives, and headings to see what the section is about. What do you think are the most important concepts in the section? How can you tell?

After you preview the section, write two questions that will help you understand or remember important concepts or facts in the section. For example, you might ask yourself

- How did the first cities grow?
- How did early civilizations form?

Find the answers to your questions as you read.

Keep asking questions about what you think will come next. Does the text answer your questions? Were you able to predict what would be covered under each heading?

Vocabulary Strategy

Using Context Clues Many English words have more than one meaning. You can use context clues to figure out the meaning of these words. For example, in the sentences below, the word *back* is used in two different ways.

He wrote his answers on the **back** of the worksheet.

From the rest of the sentence, you can figure out that *back* means "reverse side."

She asked her friends to **back** her plan.

By using context clues, you can figure out that in this sentence, *back* means "support."

Section 3 Summary

Advantages of a Settled Life

Farming was hard work. But it had advantages. People who grew their own food could stay in one place. They could store **surplus** food for later use. People could have larger families. The world's population grew quickly. About 10,000 years ago, the population of the world was about 5 million people. By 7,000 years ago, the world's population had grown to as much as 20 million.

People lived in New Stone Age farming settlements for many centuries. Settlements grew into towns. With food surpluses, people did not have to spend all their days getting food. Some people switched to other kinds of work. Some became **artisans**. They made things such as baskets, tools, pottery, and cloth. ✓

The Growth of Cities

Not all farming settlements grew into cities. Cities started in areas with rich soil. Rich soil led to large surpluses of food. People also needed plenty of drinking water and materials to build homes. Some of the earliest cities grew along rivers, such as the Nile in Egypt. Cities grew there because the soil is rich near rivers. ✓

Early cities were different from farming villages. They were larger. They had large public buildings. Some buildings were used to store crops. Other buildings were for worshipping the gods. Still others were places where people could buy and sell goods. In villages, most people were farmers. In cities, most people worked at a craft.

As the population grew, governments formed. Governments kept order. They settled disputes and managed **irrigation** projects.

Key Terms

surplus (SUR plus) *n.* more than is needed
artisan (AHR tuh zun) *n.* a worker who is especially skilled at crafting items by hand
irrigation (ihr uh GAY shun) *n.* supplying land with water through a network of canals

✓ Reading Check

What effect did food surpluses have on people living in towns?

____

____

____

✓ Reading Check

Why did cities often grow up along rivers?

____

____

____

Target Reading Skill

Ask and answer a question about how settlements grew into cities.

Question: ______________________

____

Answer: ______________________

____

Vocabulary Strategy

The word *noble* has several meanings. You may already know one of its meanings. Read the underlined sentences below. What is its meaning in this context?

___

___

___

✓ Reading Check

What skills and practices were important in the growth of early civilizations?

___

___

___

The First Civilizations

Over time, some New Stone Age societies became **civilizations**. A civilization has cities, a central government, and specialized workers. It also has writing, art, and architecture.

By 6600 B.C., artisans in Europe and Asia had learned to get copper from certain rocks. By 3000 B.C., they mixed copper and tin to make bronze. This was the start of the Bronze Age. Bronze was much harder than copper and was used to make longer-lasting weapons, tools, and shields.

Traders took precious items to faraway cities. They traded for goods that people at home wanted. Then they brought these goods back home. Around 3500 B.C., the wheel and axle were invented. Now goods could be carried farther and more easily. Merchant ships carried goods across seas and rivers. New ideas spread from one society to another. ✓

Cities developed **social classes**. In the large cities, the king was the most powerful person. Next were two other classes. One was the priests of the city's religion. The other was made up of nobles. They were government officials and military officers. Below them were artisans and merchants. At the bottom were workers and farmers. Slaves, or human beings who are owned by other people, ranked below free people.

Review Questions

1. What helped villages grow into cities?

___

___

2. What happened as societies grew into civilizations?

___

___

Key Terms

civilization (sih vuh luh ZAY shun) *n.* a society with cities, a central government, job specialization, and social classes

social class (SOH shul klas) *n.* a group of people with similar backgrounds, income, and ways of living

Chapter 1 Assessment

1. The time before writing was invented is known as
   A. oral tradition.
   B. history.
   C. prehistory.
   D. geography.

2. Historians often look at geography to tell them
   A. when people lived.
   B. about religion.
   C. about wars and rulers.
   D. how a location affected the lives of the people who lived there.

3. When did early humans cross from Asia to North America?
   A. more than a million years ago
   B. about 30,000 years ago
   C. more than 100,000 years ago
   D. 500,000 years ago

4. Which of the following describes the Old Stone Age?
   A. Early hominids learned to domesticate animals.
   B. Early hominids began to grow their own food.
   C. Some early hominids became pastoral nomads.
   D. Early hominids survived by hunting animals and gathering wild plants.

5. What did people need to grow farming settlements into cities?
   A. a large supply of slaves
   B. tame animals and grazing land
   C. rich soil, drinking water, and building materials
   D. large public buildings

Short Answer Question

How did the start of farming change people's lives?

____

____

____

____

____

Prepare to Read

Section 1
Land Between Two Rivers

Objectives

1. Find out how geography made the rise of civilization in the Fertile Crescent possible.
2. Learn about Sumer's first cities.
3. Examine the characteristics of Sumerian religion.

Target Reading Skill

Reread Rereading is a skill that can help you understand words and ideas. Rereading means to read something again. Sometimes you may not understand a word or idea the first time you read it. There may be words you do not recognize.

When this happens, rereading can help. Sometimes you may need to reread two or three times. As you reread, look for specific information that will clarify the word or idea you didn't understand. Look for connections among the words and sentences. Put together the facts that you do understand. See if you can find the main idea. Think about how the idea you don't understand relates to the main idea.

Vocabulary Strategy

Using Context to Clarify Meaning When you come across new words in your text, they are often defined for you. Sometimes the definition appears in a separate sentence or in the same sentence. Sometimes the word *or* is used to introduce the definition. Look at the following examples.

scribes, or *professional writers*

myths, or *stories about gods that explain a people's beliefs*

polytheism comes from Greek words that mean *"a belief in many gods"*

The underlined words are defined in context. In these examples, brief definitions appear in italics. Look for definitions in the context as you come across unfamiliar words in your reading.

Section 1 Summary

The first known schools were set up in the land of Sumer (SOO mur) over 4,000 years ago. They taught the new invention of writing. People who went to these schools became **scribes**. Scribes kept records that help tell the story of this early civilization.

The Geographic Setting

Sumer was located in an area called Mesopotamia (mes uh puh TAY mee uh). It had rich soil. The rivers provided water. The people who settled there became farmers, city builders, and traders.

[The word *Mesopotamia* comes from Greek words that mean "between the rivers." The region lies between the Tigris and Euphrates rivers. It is part of a larger area called the **Fertile Crescent**. This area was a very good place for growing crops.]

Each spring, the Tigris and Euphrates rivers flooded. The floods left rich topsoil on the land. Farmers grew crops in this soil. The floods did not always happen at the same time each year. Sometimes they took people by surprise. When this happened, the flood waters washed away people, animals, crops, and houses. ✓

The First Cities

Success in farming led to surpluses of food. This helped cities grow. By 3500 B.C., cities arose in Sumer, along the Tigris and Euphrates rivers.

These cities shared the same culture and language. But they did not all have the same ruler. Instead, they were independent **city-states**. Each Sumerian city acted as an independent state with its own government, its own army, and its own king.

Key Terms

scribe (skryb) *n.* someone who writes for a living
Fertile Crescent (FUR tul KRES unt) *n.* a region in Southwest Asia; site of the first civilizations
city-state (SIH tee stayt) *n.* a city with its own traditions, government, and laws; both a city and an independent state

Vocabulary Strategy

The term *Mesopotamia* is defined in context in the bracketed paragraph. Circle its definition. *Hint:* Look in the first *and* second sentences of the paragraph.

✓ Reading Check

List how flooding rivers affected people who settled in Mesopotamia.

____

____

____

Target Reading Skill

Reread this paragraph. In what ways did Sumerian cities act as independent states?

____

____

____

Life was bustling in these cities. Merchants displayed goods in outdoor market places. Streets were crowded with musicians, acrobats, beggars, and water sellers. Sumerian houses faced onto inner courtyards. On hot nights, people slept on their flat roofs. ✓

✓ Reading Check

Describe the cities of Sumer.

____

____

____

Sumerian Religion

At the heart of a Sumerian city was the ziggurat (ZIG oo rat). It was the main temple to the city's gods. Much of the town's activity took place there. A ziggurat was a tall pyramid. It had a shrine on top. Sumerians believed that gods used the ziggurat as a stairway to come down to Earth.

The people of Sumer practiced **polytheism**. Their **myths** promised that the gods would punish people who angered them. The gods would reward those who pleased them. The Sumerians honored their gods with ceremonies. The Sumerians' religion gives us an idea of what mattered to them.

Sumer's wealth led to its downfall. Sumerian city-states fought each other over land. They also fought over who could use the river water. Rulers of several city-states won and lost power. Around 2300 B.C. King Sargon of Akkad (AK ad) united the city-states of Sumer. He improved Sumer's government and army. Sumer stayed united for about 100 years. Then it split up again. After 2000 B.C., Sumer was no longer a main power. In the 1700s B.C., Babylon took control of Sumer. ✓

✓ Reading Check

What forces weakened the cities of Sumer?

____

____

____

Review Questions

1. How did Mesopotamia's geography help civilizations grow in the area?

____

____

2. Describe the religious beliefs of the people of Sumer.

____

____

Key Terms

polytheism (PAHL ih thee iz um) *n.* the belief in many gods
myth (mith) *n.* a traditional story or a legend that explains people's beliefs

Prepare to Read

Section 2
Fertile Crescent Empires

Objectives

1. Learn about the three most important empires of the Fertile Crescent.
2. Find out what characterized the Babylonian and Assyrian empires.
3. Investigate the achievements of the Persian Empire.

Target Reading Skill

Paraphrase When you paraphrase, you put something into your own words. Paraphrasing is another skill that can help you understand what you read. Putting ideas into your own words will also help you remember what you have read.

For example, look at this sentence: "King Sargon II of Assyria heard the news: Assyria had attacked the nearby kingdoms of Urartu and Zikirtu as planned." You could paraphrase it this way: "King Sargon II of Assyria learned that his country had attacked two kingdoms."

As you read, paraphrase the information following each heading.

Vocabulary Strategy

Using Context to Clarify Meaning Social studies textbooks often contain words that you may not know. Look at a word's context, or the words and sentences just before and after the word, to figure out its meaning. Clues in a word's context can include examples, explanations, or definitions. Use the graphic organizer as a guide to help you figure out the meaning of hard words.

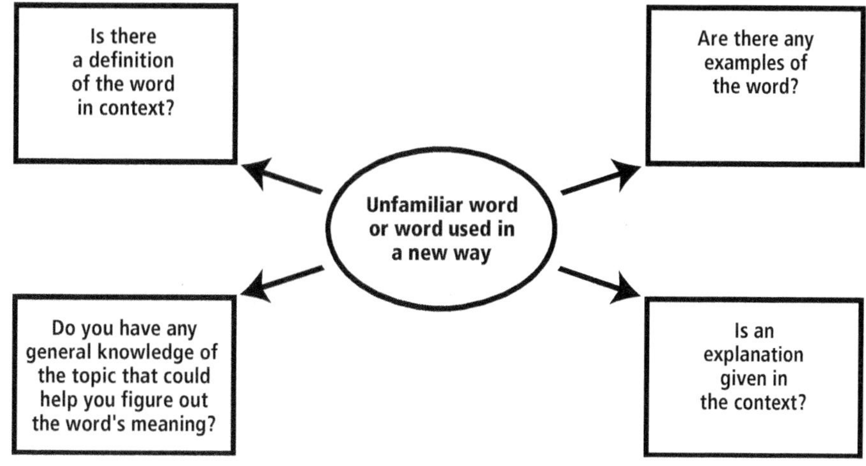

Vocabulary Strategy

As you read this section, look for at least one word that is new to you or that is used in a new way. Use the graphic organizer on the previous page to help you figure out what it means. Use the word's context for help. Write the word below, followed by a brief definition. (**Do not** use any of the Key Terms in blue.)

✓ Reading Check

Who was Hammurabi and what did he accomplish?

✓ Reading Check

How has the library at Nineveh helped us learn about early Mesopotamia?

Section 2 Summary

The Babylonian Empire

A ruler who conquered all of Mesopotamia created an **empire**. Rulers of empires gained great wealth from trade and agriculture. Hammurabi (hah muh RAH bee) created the Babylonian Empire in 1787 B.C. The city of **Babylon** was the capital of the Babylonian Empire. ✓

Babylon became a center of trade. **Caravans** stopped in Babylon on their way between Sumer and Assryia. Shoppers could buy many items in the city's **bazaars**. However, all of Babylon's wealth could not save the city. Hammurabi's empire shrank and was finally destroyed by invaders in the early 1500s B.C.

The Empire of the Assyrians

Assyria was a small kingdom north of Babylon. Assyria lay on open land so it was easily invaded. As a result, the Assyrians became skilled warriors. They decided that the best way to defend themselves was to attack others. By 650 B.C., Assyria had conquered a large empire. It stretched from the Nile River to the Persian Gulf.

The Assyrians were very good at waging war. They invented the battering ram to pound down city walls. Their armed chariots were able to slash their way through enemy troops.

Assyria's capital was Nineveh (NIN uh vuh). It was a city of great learning with a great library. It had writings from Sumer and Babylon. From these records, we know a great deal about early Mesopotamia. ✓

The people the Assyrians conquered fought against their rule. Two groups, the Medes (meedz) and Chaldeans (kal DEE unz), beat the Assyrians in 612 B.C.

Key Terms

empire (EM pyr) ***n.*** many territories and peoples controlled by one government
Babylon (BAB uh lahn) ***n.*** the capital of Babylonia; a city of great wealth and luxury
caravan (KA ruh van) ***n.*** a group of travelers journeying together
bazaar (buh ZAHR) ***n.*** a market selling different kinds of goods

Babylonia Rises Again

The Chaldeans made Babylon the center of a new empire. The New Babylonian Empire controlled the entire Fertile Crescent. King Nebuchadnezzar (neb you kud NEZ ur) II rebuilt the city. He put up huge walls to protect the city. The New Babylonian Empire was a center of learning and science. ✓

In 539 B.C., the New Babylonian Empire was conquered by the Persians. But the city of Babylon was spared.

The Persian Empire

The Persians conquered Babylon in 539 B.C. They built the largest empire the Fertile Crescent had ever known. By 490 B.C., the Persian Empire stretched from Greece to India.

Persian culture included **Zoroastrianism**. Unlike other religions at the time, Zoroastrians only worshipped one god. The Persians formed a complex government to rule their empire. They also built a network of roads that made trade with their neighbors easier.

The Persians tolerated the civilizations of the people they conquered. They also supported Babylonian science and mathematics. Persia's cultural achievements have survived to help shape our modern civilization.

Review Questions

1. What are Babylonia and Assyria?

____

____

2. How was the New Babylonian Empire created?

____

____

Key Term

Zoroastrianism (zoh roh AS tree on iz um) ***n.*** a religion that developed in ancient Persia

Target Reading Skill

Paraphrase the bracketed paragraphs on the previous page. In your paraphrase, give all the examples that show how good the Assyrians were at waging war.

____

____

____

____

✓ Reading Check

Who was Nebuchadnezzar II?

____

____

____

✓ Reading Check

How did the Persians make trade easier?

____

____

____

Prepare to Read

Section 3
The Legacy of Mesopotamia

Objectives

1. Learn about the importance of Hammurabi's Code.
2. Find out how the art of writing developed in Mesopotamia.

Target Reading Skill

Summarize You will learn more from your text if you summarize it. When you summarize text, you use your own words to restate the key points. A good summary includes important events and details. It notes the order in which the events occurred. It also makes connections between the events.

Use the table below to summarize what you will read on the next two pages.

The Legacy of Mesopotamia	
Hammurabi's Code	**The Art of Writing**

Vocabulary Strategy

Using Context to Clarify Meaning When you come across a word that you do not know, you may not need to look it up in a dictionary. In this workbook, key terms appear in **blue**. The definitions are in a box at the bottom of the page. Looking at the definition breaks up your reading. Before you do that, continue to read to the end of the paragraph. See if you can figure out what the word means from its context. Clues can include examples and explanations. Then look at the definition on the bottom of the page to see how accurate you were. Finally, reread the paragraph to make sure you understood what you read.

Section 3 Summary

Hammurabi's Code

The Babylonians thought there should be a **code** of law. This code needed to be written down. It should be applied fairly. **Hammurabi** ruled Babylonia from about 1792 to 1750 B.C. He set rules for all to follow. These rules were known as Hammurabi's Code. The code told the people how to settle disputes. The code covered all parts of life.

[Hammurabi's Code was based partly on the older Sumerian laws. It had 282 laws. The laws were grouped in categories. They included trade, labor, property, and family laws. There were laws for adopting children, practicing medicine, and hiring wagons. There were even laws dealing with wild animals.]

Hammurabi's Code was based on the idea of "an eye for an eye." In other words, the punishment should be similar to the crime. However, the code did not apply equally to all people. The punishment depended on how important the victim was. The higher the class of the victim, the worse the punishment. A person who accidentally broke a rule was just as guilty as someone who meant to break it. ✓

Hammurabi's Code is important because it was written down. With written laws, everyone knew the rules and the punishments. It was not the first time a society had set up a code of laws. But it is the first organized set that we have found.

The Art of Writing

Humans were not always able to read and write. Writing began in Mesopotamia around 3100 B.C. The Sumerians used it to keep records. The first records were about farm animals. Only a few people knew how to write. Writing was an important skill. Scribes were well respected.

Key Terms

code (kohd) *n.* an organized list of laws and rules
Hammurabi (hah muh RAH bee) *n.* the king of Babylon from about 1792 to 1750 B.C.; creator of the Babylonian empire

Target Reading Skill

Summarize the bracketed paragraph. Give the main point and two details.

Main point: ______________________

____

Detail: ______________________

____

Detail: ______________________

____

✓ Reading Check

What was Hammurabi's Code?

____

____

____

The scribes of Sumer recorded many different types of information. For example, they kept track of the payments, sales, how much food was needed to feed the army and more.

Scribes wrote on clay from the rivers. First they shaped the clay into smooth, flat surfaces called tablets. They used sharp tools to mark letters in the clay. When the clay dried, it left a permanent record.

The size and shape of a tablet depended on its use. Larger tablets were used for reference purposes. They stayed in one place. Smaller tablets were the size of letters or postcards. They were used for personal messages. They even had clay envelopes.

Writing developed over time. At first, shaped pieces of clay were used as tokens, or symbols. Tokens could be used to keep track of how many animals had been bought or sold, or how much food had been grown. By about 3100 B.C., this form of record keeping had developed into writing.

At first, people drew pictures to show what they wanted to say. Each main object had a symbol. The symbols changed when people learned to record ideas as well as facts. Eventually, scribes developed **cuneiform**. Cuneiform script could be used to stand for different languages. This was helpful in a land of many peoples. ✓

Vocabulary Strategy

From context clues, write a definition of the word *token*. Circle words or phrases in the text that helped you write your definition.

Mark the Text

____

____

____

✓ Reading Check

When, where, and how did writing first develop?

When: ______________________

Where: ______________________

How: ______________________

Review Questions

1. How does the expression "an eye for an eye" fit Hammurabi's Code?

____

____

____

2. What were some of the tasks of early Mesopotamian scribes?

____

____

____

Key Term

cuneiform (kyoo NEE uh fawrm) *n.* groups of wedges and lines used to write several languages of the Fertile Crescent

Prepare to Read

Section 4
Mediterranean Civilizations

Objectives

1. Learn how the sea power of the Phoenicians spread civilization.
2. Learn about the major events in the history of the Israelites.

Target Reading Skill

Read Ahead Reading ahead can help you understand something you are not sure of in the text. If you do not understand a word or passage, keep reading. The word or idea may be explained later. Sometimes a word is defined after it has been used. The main idea of one paragraph may be discussed in later paragraphs.

When you read the sentence about Phoenicia's resources in this section, you may not understand what a resource is. By reading ahead, you will find out that resources are things that grow or live in Phoenicia.

Vocabulary Strategy

Using Context to Clarify Meaning When you come across a new word while reading, you should look for context clues to help you figure out what the word means. The chart below shows how the subject of the section and word clues can help you determine meaning.

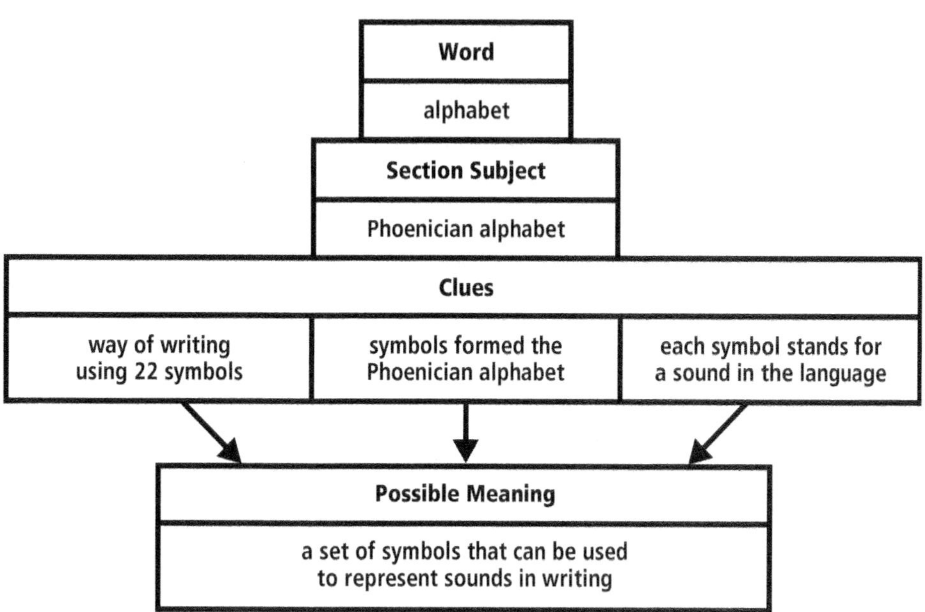

Section 4 Summary

Phoenician Sea Power

Tyre (tyr) was the major city of a region called Phoenicia (fuh NISH uh). Phoenicia was a Fertile Crescent civilization that looked west. It faced the Mediterranean Sea. There were many growing cities around this sea.

Phoenicia had few resources, but they were important. There were snails that produced a rich purple dye. The purple color was highly valued by wealthy people. There were also cedar forests. Phoenicians sold the dyed cloth and wood to neighboring peoples. ✓

The Phoenicians traded by sea to gain wealth. In time, they controlled trade in much of the Mediterranean. From about 1100 B.C. to 800 B.C., Phoenicia was a great sea power. Phoenician ships sailed as far as the Atlantic Ocean.

Trade brought goods from lands around the Mediterranean to the Phoenician cities of Tyre and Sidon (SY dun). Bazaars were full of foods and animals from faraway places.

✓ Reading Check

Circle the names of the two resources the Phoenicians first used to build their wealth.

Mark the Text

The Phoenician Alphabet

The Phoenicians used writing to help them with trade. They created a way of writing that used just 22 symbols. These symbols formed the Phoenician **alphabet**. Each of the symbols stands for a sound of the language. The alphabet is used in many languages today. English is based on this alphabet.

The Phoenician alphabet was far easier to learn than cuneiform. Many more people learned to use it. The alphabet made trade easier between people who spoke different languages. Phoenicia's sea trade helped spread the alphabet. ✓

✓ Reading Check

How did the Phoenician alphabet differ from cuneiform script?

____

____

____

The Rise of the Israelites

The Hebrews settled in the Jordan River valley. This valley was south of Phoenicia. Later they were known as the Israelites. Much of their early history comes

Key Term

alphabet (AL fuh bet) *n.* a set of symbols that represent the sounds of the language

from stories in religious books. One of these books is the Torah (TOH rah). The Torah is the Israelites' most sacred text. The Israelites greatly influenced our civilization.

The Israelites came from Mesopotamia. According to the Torah, their leader was named Abraham. The Torah says that God told Abraham to leave Mesopotamia. He taught his people to practice **monotheism**. Abraham led the Israelites to the land of Canaan (KAY nun). Then a **famine** caused them to flee to Egypt.

An Israelite named Moses led his people out of Egypt. The flight from Egypt is called the Exodus (EKS uh dus). For 40 years, the Israelites lived in the desert on the Sinai (SY ny) Peninsula. There, God gave them the Ten Commandments, a code of laws. Later, the Israelites went back to Canaan.

The Israelites united under King Saul. The next king was named David. He made Jerusalem his capital. Later the country split into two kingdoms—Israel and Judah. Judah was conquered by its neighbor, Assyria.

In 722 B.C., the Assyrians **exiled** thousands of Israelites to far-off parts of their empire. In 612 B.C., Judah was taken over by Chaldean Babylonians. In 587 B.C., the King of Judah rebelled. King Nebuchadnezzar destroyed Jerusalem and exiled the people of Judah to Babylonia. ✓

Review Questions

1. How did the Phoenicians gain their wealth and power?

____

____

2. What was the Exodus?

____

____

Key Terms

monotheism (MAHN oh thee iz um) *n.* the belief in one god
famine (FAM in) *n.* when there is so little food that people starve
exile (EK syl) *v.* to force someone to live in another country

Vocabulary Strategy

The word *Torah* is not a Key Term. But, it is defined in context. Use the chart on the first page of this section to help you find clues to clarify its meaning. Circle the words or phrases that tell you what the word *Torah* means.

Mark the Text

Target Reading Skill

The Torah says that Abraham was told to leave Mesopotamia and live elsewhere. Keep reading to see what that means.

Where did Abraham lead the Israelites?

____

____

____

✓ Reading Check

Who were the Israelites?

____

____

____

Prepare to Read

Section 5 Judaism

Objectives

1. Learn about the basic beliefs of Judaism.
2. Find out about the impact that Judaism has had on other religions.

Target Reading Skill

Summarize When you summarize, you focus on the main points. You leave out the less important details. A summary is shorter than the original text. When you summarize, keep the main ideas or facts in the correct order.

Look at the following sentence: "At the same time, religious teachers called on government leaders to temper the laws with justice and mercy." It could be summarized like this: "Religious leaders also called for justice and mercy."

As you read, pause to summarize the main ideas about Judaism.

Vocabulary Strategy

Using Context to Clarify Meaning Sometimes you may read a word you recognize, but the word does not seem to make sense in the sentence. Most words have more than one meaning. What a word means depends on its context. Look for clues in the surrounding words or sentences. For example, the word *temper* has many meanings. You cannot know what meaning the author had in mind unless you look at the context.

Some of the most common meanings of *temper* are listed in the chart below. The chart also has examples in context.

	Definitions	**Examples**
temper	mood or state of mind	She is in a good temper today.
	self-control	He lost his temper.
	a tendency to get angry	What a temper you have!
	anger or rage	She went into a temper.
	to lessen or soften	He tries to temper justice with mercy.

Section 5 Summary

The Beliefs of Judaism

To the Israelites, history and religion were closely linked. Each event showed God's plan for the Israelite people. These beliefs became the religion we know as Judaism. It was always monotheistic. It differed in other ways from the beliefs of nearby peoples.

Most ancient people thought that their gods were connected to certain places or people. The Israelites believed that God is present in all places. They believed that God knows everything. They believed that God has complete power.

[The Torah says that God promised Abraham that his people would become kings. God said they would build nations. God made a **covenant** with Abraham. The Israelites considered themselves God's "chosen people." **Moses** later renewed this covenant. He told the Israelites that God would lead them to Canaan. Canaan was the "promised land." In return, the Israelites had to obey God faithfully.]

[The Israelites believed God gave Moses the Ten Commandments. They set religious duties toward God. The Torah set many other laws. Some had to do with everyday matters. Others had to do with crimes. Like Hammurabi's Code, many laws demanded an eye for an eye. At the same time, religious teachers called on government leaders to temper the laws with justice and mercy.]

Some laws protected women. For example, mothers were to be treated with respect. But women were of lower status than men. A man who was head of a family owned his wife and children. Early on, there were some women leaders, such as the judge Deborah, who won honor and respect. But later, women were not allowed to be religious leaders.

Key Terms

covenant (KUV uh nunt) *n.* a binding agreement
Moses (MOH zuz) *n.* an Israelite leader whom the Torah says led the Israelites from Egypt to Canaan

Target Reading Skill

Summarize the first bracketed paragraph. Be sure to include the key points. Also include the important details about God's promise to the Israelites.

Key point: ____________________

Detail: ____________________

Detail: ____________________

Detail: ____________________

Vocabulary Strategy

The word *temper* is used in the second bracketed paragraph. Find it and circle it. How is it used here? Copy the correct definition from the chart at the beginning of this section.

____

____

____

The history of the Israelites tells of **prophets**. They told the Israelites what God wanted them to do. Prophets urged the Israelites to live by the idea of right and wrong. They called on the rich and powerful to protect the poor and weak. All people were equal before God. Kings were not gods. They had to obey God's law just like anyone else. ✓

✓ Reading Check

What did the prophets tell the Israelites?

____

____

____

The Effects of Judaism

People who follow Judaism are known as Jews. The Romans drove the Jews out of their homeland in A.D. 135. The Jews then scattered to many parts of the world. The Assyrians and Chaldeans had begun this **diaspora**.

Wherever they lived, Jews preserved their heritage. They lived in close communities. They obeyed their religious laws. They worshipped at their temples. They followed traditions such as Passover. These traditions helped unite Jews. ✓

✓ Reading Check

Name four ways the Jews preserved their heritage.

1. ______________________________

2. ______________________________

3. ______________________________

4. ______________________________

Judaism had an important effect on two later religions, Christianity and Islam. Both of these faiths came from the same area. Both were monotheistic. Jews, Christians, and people who follow Islam all honor Abraham, Moses, and the prophets. They share the Israelite moral point of view.

Review Questions

1. Why did the Israelites believe that they were God's chosen people?

____

____

____

2. What religious laws did the Israelites follow?

____

____

____

Key Terms

prophet (PRAHF it) ***n.*** a religious teacher who people believe speaks for God or a god

diaspora (dy AS pur uh) ***n.*** the scattering of people who have a common background or beliefs

Chapter 2 Assessment

1. *Mesopotamia* means "between the rivers." Which two rivers is it between?
   A. Sumer and Tigris rivers
   B. Phoenicia and Assur rivers
   C. Tigris and Euphrates rivers
   D. Akkadia and Sumer rivers

2. Which of these is true of the Babylonian Empire?
   A. It was created by Hammurabi.
   B. It was on open land, which was easily invaded.
   C. It had its capital at the city of Nineveh.
   D. It stretched from Greece to India.

3. Hammurabi's Code was
   A. a secret code known only to the Babylonian rulers.
   B. used as a model for the laws of the United States.
   C. based on justice and mercy.
   D. the first organized set of laws that we have found.

4. The Phoenician alphabet was
   A. the model of the alphabet used today in the United States.
   B. so hard to learn that people had to study it for years.
   C. a system that used wedges and lines scratched into clay tablets.
   D. made up of symbols that stood for objects and ideas.

5. Why did the Israelites make such a deep impact on our civilization?
   A. They ruled one of the largest empires in history.
   B. They developed the moral point of view shared by Judaism, Christianity, and Islam.
   C. They developed the alphabet that is used today.
   D. They were the only people in Southwest Asia that were never conquered by another nation.

Short Answer Question

How did the Jews preserve their heritage in exile?

____

____

____

____

____

Prepare to Read

Section 1
The Geography of the Nile

Objectives

1. Find out how the geography of the Nile changes along its course.
2. Learn about the first communities that settled along the Nile, and how people used the Nile for trade.

Target Reading Skill

Use Context Clues When you are reading, you will sometimes see an unfamiliar word. Or you may find a word you recognize, but the word is used in a new way. This is the time to look for clues to the word's meaning in the context. Context is the surrounding words, phrases, and sentences.

As you read this section, find details in the context that give clues to the meaning of *course* in the blue heading "The Course of the Nile River." What do you think *course* means?

Vocabulary Strategy

Finding Roots Many words have a few letters attached to the beginning or the end to make another word. For example, the letters *un-* may be attached at the beginning of a word. Or the letters *-ing* may be attached at the end of a word. When you remove these added letters, you end up with what is called the root. A root is a word that is used to make another word.

Attached Letters	Word	Root
un-	unwell	well
-ing	doing	do

When you come across a new word, look at it closely. See if it contains any other words that you already know. Often, you can use the root to help you figure out what the word means.

Section 1 Summary

The Course of the Nile River

The Nile River is the world's longest river. It is more than 4,000 miles (6,400 kilometers) long. It flows north to the Mediterranean Sea. It has two main sources. The Blue Nile starts in the highlands of what is now Ethiopia. The White Nile begins in East Africa and flows northward through swamps. The two rivers meet in what is now Sudan.

North of the point where the Blue Nile and White Nile meet, the Nile makes an S shape. The northern tip of the S is at the city of Aswan in Egypt. This area was **Nubia**.

Nubia has six **cataracts**. Between the first and second cataracts was Lower Nubia. It is a land of desert and granite mountains, so people lived close to the Nile for water. Between the second and sixth cataracts is Upper Nubia.

From the first cataract, the Nile passed through Upper Egypt. In the north, the Nile formed a fertile, marshy area called Lower Egypt.

Also, in the north, the Nile split into several streams that flowed into the Mediterranean Sea. These streams formed the **delta**. The water deposited sediment that was rich in minerals. Because of this, the delta contained very fertile farmland.

Every spring, waters came rushing down from the highlands. They brought a rich, fertile sediment called **silt**. Each spring, the Nile flooded the dry land and deposited a layer of thick silt. The silt was ideal for farming. Because of this dark soil, the ancient Egyptians called their land Kemet (KEH meht), "the black land." Unlike the Mesopotamians, the Egyptians usually did not have to worry about flash floods. ✓

Key Terms

Nubia (NOO bee uh) *n.* an ancient region in the Nile River Valley, now in southern Egypt and northern Sudan
cataract (KAT uh rakt) *n.* a large waterfall; any strong flood or rush of water
delta (DEL tuh) *n.* a plain at the mouth of a river, formed where flowing water deposits soil
silt (silt) *n.* fine soil found on the bottom of rivers

Target Reading Skill

If you do not know what the word *sediment* is, consider the context clues. Sediment is described as being carried by water and rich in minerals. If you read ahead, you will learn that silt is a kind of sediment. What is the meaning of *sediment*?

____

____

____

✓ Reading Check

How did the people of Nubia and Egypt benefit from the geography of the Nile?

____

____

____

Vocabulary Strategy

The words below appear in the bracketed paragraph. Each of these words contains another word that is its root. Underline the roots.

Mark the Text

useless

farming

protected

completely

traveled

Circle the words in the text. Did knowing the root help you figure out the meaning?

Beyond the fertile riverbanks was the vast desert, or "red land." These lands were useless for farming. But the rocks and hot sands protected the Egyptians and Nubians from foreign attacks. The people of Egypt and Nubia faced few invasions for about 2,000 years. But they were not completely cut off. The Nile valley was used as a highway to central Africa. People traveled to Southwest Asia by boat on the Mediterranean Sea and the Red Sea.

The Growth of Communities and Trade Along the Nile

Hunting and fishing communities may have started in Nubia around 6000 B.C. Farming communities began to appear in both Egypt and Nubia around 5000 B.C. In Egypt, villages formed near the Nile delta and in the valley. Nubia had less farmland, so people also fished in the river and hunted.

Egyptians used the Nile like a highway to carry goods for trade. Ships could float downriver because the Nile flowed north. They could sail upriver because the winds blew toward the south. Egyptians also traveled across the desert to the Red Sea or to Mesopotamia. ✓

✓ Reading Check

How did the Nile work as a highway?

____

____

____

Because of the cataracts, Nubians could travel only on land. The Nubians became famous traders of the ancient world. They brought goods from central Africa and Nubia to sell in Egypt and southwest Asia. They also brought goods home.

Review Questions

1. How did Egyptians and Nubians use the Nile River?

____

____

____

2. How did the Nile's cataracts affect Nubian trade?

____

____

____

Section 2 The Rulers of Egypt

Objectives

1. Learn the history of ancient Egyptian kingship.
2. Find out about Egypt's three kingdom periods.
3. Understand how the pharaohs ruled Egypt during the New Kingdom period.

Target Reading Skill

Use Context Clues When you need help figuring out the meaning of an unfamiliar word, use context. Context includes the surrounding words, phrases, and sentences. Sometimes the context will actually include a definition of the word.

This was a giant sphinx, *a legendary creature with a lion's body and a human head.*

Your textbook often gives you definitions of new words in the same sentence. Other times, it may be in the sentence before or after the new word. Whenever you see a new word, watch for a definition.

Vocabulary Strategy

Finding Roots Words often have a few letters added to the beginning or the end to make another word. The original word is called a root. The letters attached to the beginning or end form one or more syllables. A syllable is a group of letters that is spoken as a single sound. Below are some common syllables added to the beginning or end of words.

Beginning Syllables	Ending Syllables
de-	*-ed*
non-	*-ment*
anti-	*-ern*

What words do you know that begin or end with these syllables? What are their roots?

When you come across a new word, look to see if contains any other words that you already know.

Section 2 Summary

Egyptian Kingship

Ancient Egypt had 31 **dynasties** from about 3100 B.C. until 332 B.C. Historians group the dynasties into three kingdoms. The earliest is called the Old Kingdom. Next comes the Middle Kingdom. The last time period is the New Kingdom.

According to legend, a pharaoh, or king, named Menes (MEE neez) united Upper Egypt and Lower Egypt. That is when the first dynasty began. Menes built a city named Memphis near where Cairo (KY roh) now is. From there, he ruled over the Two Lands of Upper Egypt and Lower Egypt. This began one of the most stable civilizations in history. ✓

Egypt's **pharaohs** had **absolute power**. People thought that their pharaohs were gods.

The Three Kingdoms

Each kingdom is known for an important event or an achievement. The Old Kingdom is known for its well-run government. The pharaohs kept peace and traded with Nubia. They sent buyers to the eastern Mediterranean to find timber. Timber is trees used for building. This timber was used to build houses, boats, and furniture. Toward the end of the Old Kingdom, governors in the provinces challenged the pharaohs' rule. Egypt's unity crumbled, and the dynasties grew weak.

The Middle Kingdom returned order and reunited the country. Pharaohs spent the nation's wealth on public works, not war. Egypt grew richer. But weaker rulers followed. Then foreign invaders took over the country.

Key Terms

dynasty (DY nus tee) *n.* a series of rulers from the same family or ethnic group
pharaoh (FEHR oh) *n.* the title of the kings of ancient Egypt
absolute power (AB suh loot POW ur) *n.* complete control over someone or something

✓ Reading Check

Who was Menes and what did he do?

Target Reading Skill

The word *timber* is underlined below. If you do not know what *timber* means, look for context clues. Find a restatement of *timber*. Reread what the Egyptians used timber for. What is timber?

Vocabulary Strategy

The words below appear in the summary after the heading "The Three Kingdoms." Each of these words contains another word that is its root. Underline the roots.

government

eastern

building

reunited

Mark the Text

Circle the words in the text. Did knowing the roots help you figure out the meaning of any new words?

In time, strong Egyptian princes drove out the invaders. This was the start of the New Kingdom in 1567 B.C. The first pharaohs of the New Kingdom wanted to build an empire. They created huge armies with good weapons. One pharaoh, King Tutankhamen, became more well known after the discovery of his tomb. He had died at the young age of 18 and was buried with many precious objects. ✓

Rule During the New Kingdom

In 1504 B.C., a child named Thutmose III (thoot MOH suh) began to rule. His stepmother was made **regent**. Her name was Hatshepsut (haht SHEP soot). She had herself made pharaoh and ruled for 15 years. She created a time of great peace and economic success. When Thutmose grew up, she refused to step down. Thutmose became pharaoh after her death.

Thutmose III was one of the greatest pharaohs of the New Kingdom. His armies went east to the Euphrates River. They also went south into Nubia. But Thutmose was also an educated man. Unlike past rulers, he treated the people he defeated with mercy.

Toward the end of the New Kingdom, Egypt declined again. Civil war left Egypt weak. Then Egypt fell to Alexander the Great of Macedonia. The Macedonians ruled Egypt for about 300 years. In 51 B.C., Queen Cleopatra VII became the last Macedonian ruler. Egypt became part of the Roman Empire in 31 B.C. Egypt would not govern itself again for almost 2,000 years. ✓

Review Questions

1. What powers did Egyptians believe their kings had?

____

____

2. Describe the New Kingdom under Thutmose III.

____

____

____

Key Term

regent (REE junt) *n.* someone who rules for a child until the child is old enough to rule

✓ Reading Check

Name an important event or achievement in each of the three kingdoms.

Old Kingdom: ______________________________

____

Middle Kingdom: ______________________________

____

New Kingdom: ______________________________

____

✓ Reading Check

Why did Egypt decline during the New Kingdom period?

____

____

____

Prepare to Read

Section 3 Egyptian Religion

Objectives

1. Learn about Egyptian gods and goddesses.
2. Find out about the Egyptians' belief in the afterlife.
3. Discover how and why the pharaohs had tombs built.

Target Reading Skill

Use Context Clues Lots of words in English have more than one meaning. This can cause confusion when you read. Sometimes you come across a word you know, but it doesn't seem to make sense in the sentence. When this happens, you could look up the word in a dictionary. Or you can use context clues and your own general knowledge to figure out what the word means.

The body was then wrapped in layers of long <u>linen</u> bandages.

The word *linen* may not seem to make sense here. Perhaps you know that *linen* is used to refer to tablecloths and napkins, or to sheets and pillowcases. These are all items made of a type of cloth. Linen bandages must be bandages made of cloth.

Vocabulary Strategy

Finding Roots Syllables or groups of syllables are often added at the beginning or the end of a word. This creates a new word. The meaning of the new word is related to the original word. But it is changed in some way. For example, we can add the syllable *un-* at the beginning of *well*. The new word, *unwell*, means the opposite of the original word, *well*. It is still related to the original word because it uses the original word as its root.

When you come across a new word, look to see if it has a root. If you know the word's root, it will help you to figure out the meaning of the whole word.

Section 3 Summary

Egyptian Gods and Goddesses

Religion was very important to ancient Egyptians. They believed that their gods and goddesses controlled the natural world. So, Egyptians built temples to honor their gods. They offered them food, gifts, and prayers.

Each town had its own gods and goddesses. But all Egyptians worshiped certain gods. Over time, they all began to believe in groups of gods. The chief god of the ancient Egyptians was Amon-Re (ah mun RAY). He protected rich and poor alike. Another powerful god was Osiris (oh SY ris), the god of the living and the dead. The goddess Isis (EYE sis) was his wife. Horus, the sky god, was their son. ✓

Belief in an Afterlife

Ancient Egyptians believed in an **afterlife**. If they had pleased the gods, their spirits joined Osiris. They lived a life of ease and pleasure. However, the souls of the dead could not survive without food, clothing, and other items from this life. So, their personal items were buried with them. ✓

At first, most Egyptians were buried in the desert in shallow pits. The climate dried out the body, creating a **mummy**. The Egyptians believed the soul left the mummy, but returned to it for food offerings. The body had to be preserved so that the soul could find it. Later, the Egyptians began to preserve bodies artificially. This process was expensive. It took two or three months. Workers removed the organs. The body was filled with a natural salt and stored until it dried out. Then it was cleaned and bathed with spices. Finally, it was wrapped in layers of long linen bandages.

While the mummy was being prepared, workers carved the coffin. Pharaohs had three or four coffins that fit inside one another. The first coffin inside was usually shaped like a human body. The dead person's face was painted on the top.

Key Terms

afterlife (AF tur lyf) *n.* a life after death
mummy (MUM ee) *n.* a dead body preserved in lifelike condition

Vocabulary Strategy

The word below appears in the first sentence after the heading "Egyptian Gods and Goddesses." Underline the word's root.

Egyptians

What clue to the whole word's meaning comes from the root?

✓ Reading Check

Who was Osiris?

✓ Reading Check

Why did ancient Egyptians bury their dead with food and personal items?

The Pharaohs' Tombs

The earliest royal tombs were made of mud brick. The pharaohs of the Fourth Dynasty built the largest and most famous tombs. These were the **pyramids**. The largest is the Great Pyramid in **Giza**. It was built for Khufu (KOO foo), the second king of this dynasty.

Pyramid building took great organization. For example, the Great Pyramid is made up of more than 2 million stones. The average weight is 5,000 pounds (2,270 kilograms). Each stone had to be hauled up the side and put into its place.

It could take more than 20 years to build a pyramid. First a site was selected on the west bank of the Nile. Engineers set the pyramid square with the main points of the compass. Workers then cut the building blocks. Stone for the inside came from nearby. But fine stone for the outside came from farther away. Some stone came by boat.

Sleds, wooden rollers, and levers were used to get the blocks into place. They dragged and pushed the blocks up ramps of packed rubble. It was dangerous work. Men were killed in accidents. But the workers believed that their work was important. It meant the pharaoh had a place in the afterlife. ✓

Target Reading Skill

What does *hauled* mean in the bracketed paragraph? Look for context clues in the text.

___

✓ Reading Check

Why did the Egyptians build pyramids?

___

Review Questions

1. What was the purpose of a mummy for ancient Egyptians?

___

2. How do we know that the afterlife was important to the ancient Egyptians?

___

Key Terms

pyramid (PIH ruh mid) *n.* a huge building with four sloping triangular-shaped sides; built as royal tombs in Egypt
Giza (GEE zuh) *n.* an ancient Egyptian city; the site of the Great Pyramid

Prepare to Read

Section 4 Ancient Egyptian Culture

Objectives

1. Find out how ancient Egyptians lived everyday.
2. Learn about writing in ancient Egypt.
3. Discover Egyptian achievements in science and medicine.

Target Reading Skill

Use Context Clues You have learned that using context can help you figure out the meaning of an unfamiliar word. The words, phrases, and sentences around a word can provide clues.

In some cases, cause-and-effect clues can help you understand the meaning of the word. In the following sentence, a cause-and-effect clue points to the meaning of *scattered*:

The farmer <u>scattered</u> the seeds, which flew and landed all around.

Ask: What caused the seeds to land all around? What do you think *scattered* means?

Vocabulary Strategy

Finding Roots Often, syllables or groups of syllables are added at the beginning or the end of a word to make a new word. The meaning of the new word is related to the original word. But it is changed in some way. It is still related to the original word because it uses the original word as its root.

In some cases, the spelling changes slightly when a word becomes a root. Often, a final *e* is dropped when a new ending is added to a word. For example, if we add the ending *y* to the word *ease*, it is spelled *easy* (and **not** *easey*!).

If you keep this in mind, you can see that the word *writing* contains the root *write*.

Section 4 Summary

The Lives of the Egyptians

Egyptian society was built like a pyramid.

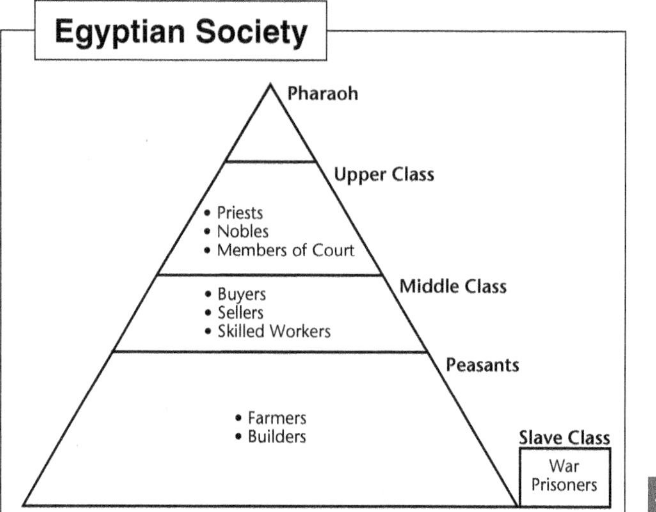

During the flood season, peasants worked on roads, temples, and other buildings. After the floods, they farmed the land of the rich or their own land.

Women had most of the rights of men. They could own property, run businesses, and travel. Even slaves had rights. The could own personal items and inherit land. They could also be set free.

Writing in Ancient Egypt

The ancient Egyptians had a special way of writing. They used **hieroglyphs** to keep records of the kingdom's growing wealth.

At first, the Egyptians wrote on clay and stone. But then they made something better—**papyrus**. Inner stalks of the papyrus plant were cut into narrow strips. Next, strips were placed side by side in one layer. Another layer of strips was placed crosswise. Then, strips were soaked, pounded flat, and dried. Finally, sap from the plant glued the strips together.

Key Terms

hieroglyphs (HY ur oh glifs) n. pictures and other written symbols that stand for ideas, things, or sounds

papyrus (puh PY ruhs) *n.* an early form of paper made from a reed plant found in the marshy areas of the Nile delta

Vocabulary Strategy

The words below appear after the heading "The Lives of the Egyptians." Each of these words contains a root. Underline the root.

worked

buildings

businesses

Mark the Text

Circle the word in the text. Did knowing any of these roots help you figure out its meaning in context?

✓ Reading Check

How was Egyptian society organized?

______

______

______

Target Reading Skill

What does *sap* mean in the underlined sentence below? Look for cause-and-effect clues in the text. Sap from the plant glues the strips of papyrus together. What is sap?

______

______

______

After the A.D. 400s, people had forgotten what the symbols of hieroglyphs meant. But, in 1799 a soldier dug up a large black stone near the Nile. Two parts of the stone had different forms of hieroglyphs. A third part had Greek letters. In the 1820s, a French scholar used the Greek letters to figure out the meanings of the hieroglyphs. This opened up a new window onto the world of ancient Egypt. The stone is called the Rosetta Stone because it was found near the city of Rosetta. ✓

Science and Medicine

As farmers, the ancient Egyptians needed to know when the Nile would flood every year. Their **astronomers** helped by figuring out the length of a year—365 days. ✓

The Egyptians had good math skills. Mathematics helped them measure rock to build pyramids. They were also able to measure the area of a plot of land.

The ancient Egyptians studied the human body. They learned to perform surgery and set broken bones. They also created medicines from plants.

Review Questions

1. How were the lives of Egypt's peasants ruled by the seasons?

____

____

____

2. What areas of science and medicine did the ancient Egyptians study?

____

____

____

Key Term

astronomer (uh STRAHN uh mur) *n.* a scientist who studies the stars and other objects in the sky

✓ Reading Check

Why was the Rosetta Stone an important discovery?

____

____

____

✓ Reading Check

Why was it important for the Egyptians to know the length of their year?

____

____

____

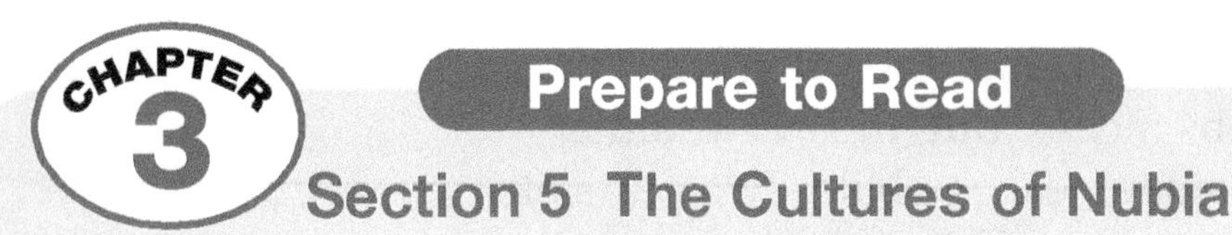

Section 5 The Cultures of Nubia

Objectives

1. Look at the relationship between Nubia and Egypt.
2. Learn about the Nubian kingdoms centered in Kerma, Napata, and Meroë.

Target Reading Skill

Use Context Clues Context refers to the words, phrases, or sentences before or after the word. Context can offer clues to the meaning of words that are new to you.

One strategy for understanding unfamiliar words is to use synonyms. A synonym is a word that has a similar meaning.

Taharka received the ultimate prize, the greatest honor possible.

The word *greatest* is a synonym for *ultimate*. As you read, look for synonyms and other context clues.

Vocabulary Strategy

Finding Roots You now know that syllables or groups of syllables can be added at the beginning or the end of a word to make a new word. The meaning of the new word is related to the original word. But it is changed in some way.

In some cases, the spelling changes slightly when a word becomes a root. Often, a *y* at the end of a word is changed to *i* when the word becomes a root. For example, if we add the ending *-ly* to the word *easy*, it is spelled *easily* (and **not** *easyly*!).

If you keep this in mind, you can see that the word *geographic* comes from *geography*.

Section 5 Summary

Nubia and Egypt

For years, Nubia and Egypt were mostly peaceful neighbors. Egypt needed Nubia for its gold, copper, and iron **ores**. Also, **Lower Nubia** was a connection for goods between central Africa and Egypt. In time, powerful kingdoms arose in **Upper Nubia**. The most powerful were in the cities of Kerma, Napata, and Meröe. These kingdoms wanted land controlled by Egypt. The Nubians were ruled by the Kushites, people of southern Nubia. ✓

The Kerma Culture

When Egypt grew weak, the Kushites took control. By about 1600 B.C., the Kushite kingdom had expanded from the Nubian city of Kerma (KUR muh) into parts of Egypt. These Nubians are called the Kerma culture. Their kingdom lasted nearly 500 years.

Kerma was rich from its trading with central Africa. It was noted for its **artisans**. These craftsmen made beautiful pottery. Like Egyptians, the people of Kerma spent their resources on royal burials. They built mounds of earth as large as football fields. Inside, the kings' bodies were surrounded by gold, ivory, and jewels. ✓

Egypt grew stronger around the 1500s B.C. After 50 years of war, Egypt took control of part of Nubia. Egypt ruled this part of Nubia for about 700 years. During that period, the Nubians adopted many Egyptian ways. They even began to worship Egyptian gods along with their own. The two cultures began to mix.

✓ Reading Check

Why did Nubia and Egypt become rivals?

____

____

____

Target Reading Skill

Do you know what *artisan* means? Look for context clues. What does the word mean?

____

____

____

✓ Reading Check

What were some features of Kerma?

____

____

____

Key Terms

ore (awr) *n.* a mineral or a combination of minerals mined for the production of metals

Lower Nubia (LOH ur NOO bee uh) *n.* the region of ancient Nubia between the First and Second Nile cataracts

Upper Nubia (UP ur NOO bee uh) *n.* the region of ancient Nubia between the Second and Sixth Nile cataracts

artisan (AHR tuh zun) *n.* a worker who is skilled in crafting goods by hand

Vocabulary Strategy

The words below appear under the heading "Napata and Meröe." Each of these words contains a root. Underline the roots. If the spelling of the root has been changed, write the correct root after the word.

controlled

Nubians

moving

allowed

hieroglyphics

✓ Reading Check

How did the people of Meroë use iron ore?

____

____

____

Napata and Meroë

In the late 700s B.C., Egypt grew weak again. At the same time, the Kushites had grown strong. From their city Napata (nuh PAY tuh), the Kushites moved back into Egypt. They made their capital first in Thebes, then in Memphis. Soon, they controlled all of Egypt. The pharaohs of Egypt's Twenty-fifth Dynasty were Nubians. But their rule did not last very long. About 660 B.C., they were forced back to Napata. Then they moved their capital south to Meroë (MEHR oh ee). They never again controlled Egyptian land.

After moving as far from Egypt as possible, the Nubians started over. Meroë became the center of an empire that included much of Nubia and central Africa. Meroë's desert had large deposits of iron ore. The Nubians used the ore to make iron weapons and tools. Iron plows allowed them to grow large supplies of food. Iron weapons allowed them to control trade routes. Meroë became rich from trade. ✓

The Meroë culture created its own type of hieroglyphics. So far, scholars have not been able to understand the symbols. Because of this, Meroë is largely a mystery. It began to weaken in the A.D. 200s. Later, it fell to another African kingdom. But parts of Nubian culture such as braided hairstyles, clothing, pottery, furniture, and jewelry, are still found in present-day Sudan.

Review Questions

1. What was the relationship between Egypt and Nubia?

____

____

____

2. How is the history of Napata tied to Egypt?

____

____

____

Chapter 3 Assessment

1. The Nile River flows
   A. north for about 4,000 miles.
   B. south to the Mediterranean Sea.
   C. north to the Red Sea.
   D. south.

2. The three kingdoms of ancient Egypt refer to
   A. Upper Egypt, Lower Egypt, and Nubia.
   B. the three main time periods into which Egypt's history is grouped.
   C. Kerma, Napata, and Meroë.
   D. periods of trouble between Egypt's dynasties.

3. The chief Egyptian god was
   A. Amon-Re.
   B. Horus.
   C. Isis.
   D. Osiris.

4. Which of the following describes the Egyptian class system?
   A. It was shaped like a pyramid.
   B. A person could not rise to a higher class.
   C. Only pharaohs could own property and inherit land.
   D. It was very rigid and people could not rise to a higher class.

5. Which of the following Nubian cultures created a system of hieroglyphic writing?
   A. Egypt
   B. Kerma
   C. Napata
   D. Meroë

Short Answer Question

Describe the locations of Upper and Lower Egypt, and Upper and Lower Nubia on the course of the Nile River.

____

____

____

____

____

Prepare to Read

Section 1 The Indus and Ganges River Valleys

Objectives

1. Learn about India's geographic setting.
2. Find out about life in an ancient city of the Indus River valley.
3. Learn about the rise of a new culture in the Indus and Ganges river valleys.

Target Reading Skill

Identify Causes and Effects A cause makes something happen. It is the reason that something happens. An effect is what happens. It is the result of the cause. As you read, pause to ask yourself what happened. The answer to that question is the effect. Then ask yourself why it happened. The answer to that question is the cause.

For example, millions of years ago India's landmass crashed into Asia. Think of this as the cause. The effect was the formation of the Himalaya Mountains.

Seeing causes and effects helps you understand how events are connected. It helps you understand why things happen as they do.

Vocabulary Strategy

Recognizing Compound Words When you come across a new word, you may be able to figure out what it means if you break it down into parts. For example, if you did not know what the word *snowball* means, you could break it down into its parts: *snow* and *ball*. A snowball is a ball of snow. Many words in English are made by combining two or more words. Such words are referred to as *compound words*. As you read, use what you know about compound words to help you understand new words.

Here are some common words that are made up of two words:

anybody	*homeland*	*seashore*
baseball	*landform*	*skyscraper*
countryside	*mainland*	*southwest*
downtown	*mountaintop*	*waterway*
farmland	*northeast*	*worldwide*

Section 1 Summary

India's Geographic Setting

The land of India sticks out from the rest of Asia into the Indian Ocean. India is part of a **subcontinent**. The Himalayas and the Hindu Kush mountain range cut India off from Asia. Like these mountains, the bodies of water around India separated it from surrounding areas. Because of this, India had little contact with the rest of the world for many years.

India's climate is ruled by **monsoons**, or strong seasonal winds. From October to May, the winter monsoon blows from the northeast. It spreads dry air across the country. The summer monsoon comes in the middle of June. It picks up moisture from the Indian Ocean. The people rely on summer monsoons for rain. If the monsoon is late or weak, crops die and there is famine. If there is too much rain, rivers may flood. ✓

The first people of northern India probably came through openings in the Hindu Kush mountains. Great rivers rise in the mountains. The Indus (IN dus) River flows into the Arabian Sea. The Ganges (GAN jeez) River flows into the Bay of Bengal. The rivers let farmers grow crops in the plains of northern India.

Life in the Indus River Valley

The Indus Valley had rich soil. With surplus food, the number of people grew. From around 2500 B.C. to 1500 B.C., cities grew up in the valley. One large city was Mohenjo-Daro (moh HEN joh DAH roh). It was on the banks of the Indus River.

Mohenjo-Daro was well planned. It was built above ground level to protect it from floods. Homes and shops were on one side of the city. Public buildings were on the other side. A wall protected the city's most important buildings. These buildings included the **citadel**.

Key Terms

subcontinent (SUB kahn tih nunt) ***n.*** a large piece of land that sticks out from a continent
monsoon (mahn SOON) ***n.*** a strong wind that blows across East Asia at certain times of the year
citadel (SIT uh del) ***n.*** a fortress in a city

Target Reading Skill

Mark the Text

Circle one cause described in the bracketed paragraph and underline its effect.

✓ Reading Check

How do winter monsoons differ from summer monsoons?

✓ Reading Check

Describe the city plan for Mohenjo-Daro.

____

____

____

Mohenjo-Daro had a means of draining water from the land. Clay pipes under the streets sent waste away from the city. Canals ran next to the Indus River. They helped to keep flood water from the city. ✓

Around 2000 B.C., the people of the Indus Valley began to leave their land. From 2000 B.C. to 1500 B.C., newcomers from the north came to the area.

A New Culture Arises

The new people were called Aryans (AYR ee uhnz). They **migrated** from their homelands in central Asia. They were nomadic herders. Local people adopted the Aryans' language. They also adopted some of their beliefs. A new mixed Aryan culture began.

Vocabulary Strategy

Mark the Text

Remember to look for compound words as you read. There are two on this page. As you find each one, draw a line between the two words that form the compound.

Then write the words you found on the lines below.

1. __________________________

2. __________________________

This new culture first started in the northern Indus Valley. It spread into the Ganges Valley to the east. By about 800 B.C., the people of northern India had learned to make tools and weapons of iron. With iron axes, they cleared the thick rain forests.

Aryan society was grouped into three classes. Priests, called Brahmans, performed religious services. Below them were warriors and nobles. Next came the artisans and merchants. Finally, a fourth class of people made up of farm workers, laborers, and servants was formed.

This division of classes is the **caste** system. People had to stay in the caste of their parents. Each caste had many groups. People did the same work as their parents and other members of their group. ✓

✓ Reading Check

How was Aryan society organized?

____

____

____

Review Questions

1. How do the monsoons affect India's climate?

____

____

2. Who were the Aryans?

____

____

Key Terms

migrate (MY grayt) *v.* to relocate; to move from one place and settle in another
caste (kast) *n.* a social class of people

Prepare to Read

Section 2 Hinduism in Ancient India

Objectives

1. Find out about the beginnings of Hinduism.
2. Learn about the basic beliefs of Hinduism.
3. Examine the practice of Hinduism.

Target Reading Skill

Recognize Cause-and-Effect Signal Words As you read, watch for clues that show cause and effect. Often, a word will give you a signal that what is being described is either a cause or an effect. Words such as *affect*, *as a result*, and *from* signal a cause or effect.

In the following example, *from* signals a cause: "*From* this blend of ideas and beliefs came one of the world's oldest living religions, Hinduism." The cause is a blend of ideas and beliefs. The effect is Hinduism.

As you read, look for signals that explain other causes and effects.

Vocabulary Strategy

Using Prefixes and Roots A prefix is one or more syllables attached to the beginning of a word to make a new word. The word it is attached to is known as the root. When a prefix is added to a root, the new word has a new meaning. The meaning of the prefix is added to the meaning of the root.

Some common prefixes are listed below, along with their meanings and examples. Notice that some of them have more than one meaning. Learning to identify prefixes, and knowing what they mean, will help you understand what you read.

Prefix	Meaning	Example
in-, im-	in, into, within, on, toward	inject, immigrate
non-	not	nontoxic
pre-	before	prehistory
re-	again	reread

Section 2 Summary

Vocabulary Strategy

The words below appear in this section. Each word contains a prefix. Underline the prefix in each word.

reborn

nonviolence

Mark the Text

Now look at the chart on the previous page. Use the chart to find the prefix's meaning. Then, add the meaning of the prefix to the meaning of the root.

1. Reborn means ______________________________

2. Nonviolence means ______________________________

✓ Reading Check

List the most important Hindu gods.

1. ______________________
2. ______________________
3. ______________________

The Beginnings of Hinduism

Aryan culture mixed with India's existing cultures. From this blend of ideas and beliefs came one of the world's oldest living religions, Hinduism. It has picked up beliefs from other religions in its 3,500 years. It became very complex. Hindus believe that there are many ways of coming to god.

Hinduism is one of the world's major religions. More than 850 million people in India follow it today. Its beliefs have influenced people of many religions. But it is different from other major world religions. There is no one founder. Hindus worship many gods and goddesses. But they believe in one single spiritual power. This power is called **brahman**.

The gods and goddesses of Hinduism stand for different parts of brahman. The three most important gods are Brahma the Creator, Vishnu the Preserver, and Shiva is the Destroyer. Each one takes many forms. These forms are called **avatars**. ✓

Hindus believe that Brahma created Earth and all that is on it. But he is not as widely worshipped as Vishnu and Shiva. Vishnu is kind. He tries to protect humans. Shiva is responsible for both the creative and destructive forces in the universe. Hindu gods have families. Many Hindus worship Shiva's wife, Shakti.

The Teachings of Hinduism

All Hindus share certain beliefs. They are in religious writings. One of these is the Upanishads (oo PAN uh shadz). *Upanishad* means "sitting near a teacher."

One of the shared ideas is **reincarnation**. Hindus believe that when a person dies, the soul is reborn in another living thing. They believe that every living thing has a soul.

Key Terms

brahman (BRAH mun) *n.* a single spiritual power that Hindus believe lives in everything
avatar (av uh TAHR) *n.* a Hindu god or goddess in human or animal form
reincarnation (ree in kahr NAY shun) *n.* rebirth of the soul in the body of another living thing

Hindus believe that a person's actions in this life affect his or her fate in the next. Good behavior is rewarded. Bad behavior is punished. Faithful followers of Hinduism will be born into a higher position. Those who have been bad may be born into a lower caste. They may even return as an animal. A perfect life may free a soul from the cycle of death and rebirth. As a result, this person's soul is united with brahman. ✓

To do this, a person must obey his or her **dharma**. The duties of dharma depend on a person's class, job, and age. **Ahimsa**, or nonviolence, is also important. To Hindus, all people and things are part of brahman. They must be treated with respect. That is why many Hindus do not eat meat. They try not to hurt living things.

The Practice of Hinduism

Hindus believe that there are many paths to the truth. They may worship in different ways. One way is by practicing yoga (YOH guh). Yoga means union. Hindus believe yoga exercises help free the soul from the cares of the world. It helps the soul unite with brahman. There are many yogas that lead to brahman. Physical activity is one yoga. Another is selfless deeds, such as giving to the poor. ✓

Review Questions

1. How did the early Aryan culture influence Hinduism?

___

2. What does Hinduism teach about the path to truth?

___

Key Terms

dharma (DAHR muh) *n.* the religious and moral duties of Hindus
ahimsa (uh HIM sah) *n.* the Hindu idea of nonviolence

Target Reading Skill

What does *As a result* signal?

___

✓ Reading Check

According to Hindu belief, what happens to a person's soul after death?

___

✓ Reading Check

How is yoga practiced by Hindus?

___

Prepare to Read

Section 3 The Beginnings of Buddhism

Objectives

1. Learn about the Buddha and his teachings.
2. Find out how Buddhism was received inside and outside India.

Target Reading Skill

Recognizing Multiple Causes A cause makes something happen. An effect is what happens. Often, an effect can have more than one cause. For example, in the story that begins this section, Gautama sees three events that cause him to change his life. Can you identify the three causes?

Looking for more than one cause will help you fully understand why something happened. As you read this section, look for other things that have multiple causes.

Vocabulary Strategy

Using Roots and Suffixes A suffix is one or more syllables attached to the end of a word to make a new word. The word it is attached to is known as the root. When a suffix is added to a root, the new word has a new meaning. The meaning of the suffix is added to the meaning of the root.

Some common suffixes are listed below, along with their meanings and examples. Notice that some have more than one meaning. Learning to identify suffixes, and knowing what they mean, will help you understand what you read.

Suffix	Meaning	Example
-ern	of or related to	eastern
-ing	an action; result of an action	dancing; drawing
-ism	act or practice of; teaching	terrorism; socialism
-less	without	treeless
-ly	in a certain manner; like	seriously; manly
-ness	state or quality	happiness

Section 3 Summary

Buddhists believe that a young Hindu prince once lived a life of luxury in northern India. He had never seen old age, sickness, or death. Then, he traveled outside the palace walls. He saw an old man. He saw a man who was very sick. He saw a dead body being carried to a funeral.

The young man gave up his life of ease. He wanted to find the causes of human suffering. The young man was Siddhartha Gautama (sih DAHR tuh GOW tuh muh). What he learned after seven years of wandering led to the start of Buddhism.

The Buddha and His Teachings

Gautama travelled in the 500s B.C. and looked for the meaning of life. At first, he studied with Hindu thinkers. But their ideas did not satisfy him.

Gautama decided to look inside himself for understanding. He began to **meditate**. Meditation was an ancient Hindu practice. After 49 days, he found the answers he had been looking for. He traveled across India and shared what he had learned. His followers called him the Buddha (BOO duh), or "Enlightened One." His teachings became known as Buddhism.

Buddhism teaches people to follow the Eightfold Path, also called the Middle Way. By doing this, a person avoids extreme pleasure or extreme unhappiness.

Buddha taught that selfish desires cause humans to suffer. To end suffering, people must give up these selfish desires for wealth, power, and pleasure. Instead, they must follow the Eightfold Path. Buddhists must learn to be wise, to behave correctly, and to develop their minds.

Key Term

meditate (MED uh tayt) *v.* to focus the mind inward in order to find spiritual awareness or relaxation

Vocabulary Strategy

Mark the Text

The word *northern* appears in the paragraph to the left. Find the word as you read and underline the suffix. Then, on the line below, write a definition of the word using the information in the chart on the previous page.

Northern means ____________

____

____

Target Reading Skill

Circle the factors in the bracketed paragraph that affect a Buddhist trying to reach nirvana.

Mark the Text

✓ Reading Check

Why do Buddhists try to follow the Middle Way?

____

____

____

✓ Reading Check

What other countries has Buddhism spread to?

____

____

____

To find this Middle Way, people must act unselfishly. They must treat people fairly. They must tell the truth at all times. They should also avoid violence and the killing of any living thing. By following the Buddha's path, their sufferings would end. They would find **nirvana**. They would not be reincarnated. ✓

Buddhism taught that all people are equal. Anyone could follow the path to nirvana. This idea appealed to many people. Like other religions, Buddhism has priests. People of any social class can be a priest or monk. The Buddha encouraged his followers to establish monasteries. There they would learn, meditate, and teach. He urged monks to become **missionaries**.

Buddhism Inside and Outside India

For many years, Buddhism and Hinduism lived side by side in India. Both share a number of basic ideas. Both believe that it is wrong to harm living things. Both value nonviolence. However, Buddhists do not accept the sacred texts of Hinduism.

Buddhism spread all over Asia. It took root in China and grew there. Buddhist monasteries were centers of religious thought in China. From China, Buddhism spread to Korea and Japan. Today, it is part of the cultures of countries such as Japan, China, and Vietnam. ✓

Review Questions

1. How did Siddhartha Gautama look for the cause of human suffering?

____

____

2. What are some of the similarities between Hinduism and Buddhism?

____

____

Key Terms

nirvana (nur VAH nuh) *n.* the lasting peace that Buddhists seek by giving up selfish desires
missionary (MISH un ehr ee) *n.* a person who spreads his or her religious beliefs to others

Prepare to Read

Section 4 Empires of Ancient India

Objectives

1. Learn about the rise of the Maurya Empire.
2. Understand the effects of Asoka's leadership on the Maurya Empire.

Target Reading Skill

Understand Effects Remember that a cause makes something happen. The effect is what happens as a result of the cause. Just as an effect can have more than one cause, a cause can have more than one effect. You can find effects by answering the question, "What happened?" If there are several answers to that question, the cause had more than one effect.

Look at the last paragraph under the heading "The Rise of the Maurya Empire" in the next page. What were the effects of wealth on the Maurya Empire?

Vocabulary Strategy

Using Word Parts Sometimes when you come across a new word, you can figure out what it means if you break it down into parts. If a word contains a prefix or suffix, look for the root. The root is the word that the prefix or suffix is attached to. Take the meanings of the root and prefix or suffix and add them together. Then you will have found the meaning of the new word.

Often, when a prefix or a suffix is added to a root, the root's spelling is changed.

A final vowel, such as *a* or *e*, may be dropped: *Buddha* + *-ism* = *Buddhism*

A final *y* may change to *i*: *happy* + *-ly* = *happily*

A final consonant may be doubled: *war* + *-ing* = *warring*

Some words have more than one prefix or suffix. Some words have both prefixes and suffixes. In those cases, strip off the prefix or suffix one at a time until you can figure out what the word means.

Section 4 Summary

Around 321 B.C., Chandragupta (chun druh GOOP tuh) Maurya began his rule in northeastern India. His small kingdom grew into the huge **Maurya Empire**.

The Rise of the Maurya Empire

Before Chandragupta came to power, India was made up of a number of states. These states fought each other. Chandragupta's armies overthrew kingdoms along the Ganges River. Then they turned west, to the Indus River valley. Within a few years, he controlled most of north and central India.

Chandragupta thought that a ruler must have absolute power. According to legend, one of his advisors gave him a book of advice called *Arthasastra*. The book urged kings to control their people. It said kings should keep an army of spies to inform on them.

Chandragupta commanded a huge army. Under him, the empire became wealthy. Much of its wealth came from farming. But the Maurya Empire also traded with faraway lands. Some of these lands were Greece, Rome, and China.

As his rule continued, Chandragupta began to fear that he would be killed. According to one story, near the end of his life, he left the throne to his son. He became a monk and starved himself to death fasting and praying.

His rule was harsh. But Chandragupta used his wealth to improve his empire. New irrigation systems brought water to farmers. Trees were cut down, and more food was grown. Government officials promoted crafts and mining. New roads made trade with foreign lands easier. Chandragupta brought order and peace to his people. ✓

Asoka's Leadership

Chandragupta's grandson, Asoka, built the greatest empire India had ever seen. His rule ended in 232 B.C.

Key Term

Maurya Empire (MOWR yuh EM pyr) *n.* Indian empire founded by Chandragupta, including most of northern and central India

Vocabulary Strategy

There are several words with suffixes in the bracketed paragraph. Circle each word in the paragraph that has a suffix.

Mark the Text

✓ Reading Check

What kind of ruler was Chandragupta?

Asoka ruled for more than 35 years. His empire included much of India. At first, he was as warlike as his grandfather. In about 261 B.C., he won a fight in Kalinga. Thousands of people died there. He was very sad about the deaths. He gave up war. He freed his prisoners. Later, he **converted** to Buddhism. ✓

Asoka practiced and preached the Buddha's teachings. He thought of his people as his children. He cared about them. He had hospitals built throughout the land. He had wells dug along roads so that travelers and animals would have water.

Asoka wanted to share the Buddha's message with all people in his empire. He gave moral advice. Asoka practiced **tolerance** toward Hindus. He also sent Buddhist missionaries to spread Buddhism to Sri Lanka, China, Southeast Asia, Korea, and Japan.

After Asoka died, the Maurya Empire weakened and split apart. Conflicts among small states and foreign invaders occurred during this time. However, from A.D. 320 to 540, the Gupta Dynasty built an empire across northern India.

Under the Guptas, India enjoyed a rich culture. Indians developed advanced schools of philosophy. They also invented the decimal point and the system of numbers that we use today.

Review Questions

1. How did Chandragupta build the Maurya Empire?

____

____

____

2. What were some of Asoka's accomplishments?

____

____

____

Key Terms

convert (kun VURT) *v.* to change one's beliefs
tolerance (TAHL ur uns) *n.* freedom from prejudice

Target Reading Skill

What effects did the Battle of Kalinga have on Asoka's life?

____

____

____

✓ Reading Check

What event caused Asoka to become a Buddhist?

____

____

____

Chapter 4 Assessment

1. India is separated from the rest of Asia by the Himalayas and
   A. the Ganges River.
   B. the Indus River.
   C. the Hindu Kush mountain range.
   D. the Great Wall of China.

2. As Aryans migrated into the northern Indus Valley, local people adopted their
   A. children.
   B. language and domesticated dogs.
   C. language and beliefs.
   D. beliefs and citadel style buildings.

3. Which of the following is NOT true of Hindu gods and goddesses?
   A. They are all kindly and concerned with human matters.
   B. They stand for different parts of the same spirit.
   C. They can take many different forms.
   D. They have their own families.

4. Buddhism teaches that all people should
   A. pursue pleasure.
   B. follow The Twelvefold Path.
   C. be part of a caste system.
   D. regard themselves as equal.

5. Which of the following happened under Chandragupta's rule?
   A. Buddhism was carried throughout the empire.
   B. Government officials promoted crafts and mining.
   C. Hospitals were built throughout the empire.
   D. Wells were dug along roads so that travelers and animals would not go thirsty.

Short Answer Question

What are some ways in which Hinduism and Buddhism differed from each other?

____

____

____

____

____

Prepare to Read

Section 1 The Geography of China's River Valleys

Objectives

1. Examine the geography of ancient China.
2. Find out about early civilization in China.
3. Learn about the importance of family ties in early China.

Target Reading Skill

Identify Main Ideas It is hard to remember every detail that you read. Good readers are able to find the main ideas of what they read. The main idea is the most important point. It includes all the other points, or details.

To find the main idea of a paragraph, read it through once. Then ask yourself what is the paragraph about. Do all the sentences center on the same point? If so, you've found your main idea. Sometimes it is stated in the first sentence or two.

The main idea of the paragraph below is underlined:

> The family was the center of early Chinese society. It was more important than each person or the nation. The family came first.

As you read, look for the main ideas of paragraphs.

Vocabulary Strategy

Recognizing Signal Words Signal words are words or phrases that prepare you for what is coming next.

There are different kinds of signal words. Often signal words tell you when things happen. Some of these signal words are:

then	*later*
when	*around* (followed by a date)
in time	*in* (followed by a date)
earlier	*as early as* (followed by a date)

Section 1 Summary

The Geography of Ancient China

Ancient China covered a large area. The climate, soil, landforms, and waterways were different in each region.

The North China Plain is in East Asia. It is made of soil deposits from the Huang (hwahng) River. Northern China has only a brief summer monsoon. There is not much rain at other times. The climate is very dry. People here depend on rivers to survive.

The climate in southern China is warm and wet. Monsoons bring heavy rains from March to September. Light rain falls the rest of the year.

Mountains and seas separated China from other lands. The Chinese had little contact with other civilizations. The Chinese thought that they lived at the center of the world so they called themselves the Middle Kingdom.

China's rivers flooded each spring. This brought fresh, fertile topsoil to the land. China's first farming villages developed along its rivers. Civilization began along the Huang. It later spread to the wetter south, along the Chang, China's longest river.

The Huang is China's second-longest river. The word *huang* means "yellow" in Chinese. It is called the "Yellow River" because of the **loess** that it carries. When it floods, it deposits loess on the surrounding plain. Here, the Chinese grow a grain called millet.

The Chinese people also call the Huang "China's Sorrow." Its floods could be very destructive. Early Chinese people built **dikes** to help control flooding. ✓

Early Civilization in China

China's first farming settlements were in the Huang Valley. They may have began as early as 5000 B.C. Later on, they grew into civilizations.

Key Terms

loess (LOH es) *n.* yellow-brown soil
dike (dyk) *n.* a wall that controls or holds back water

Vocabulary Strategy

As you read this section's summary, look for the following signal words that indicate when something happened. Circle the signal words when you find them.

Mark the Text

when

as early as

later on

around 1760 B.C.

much later

✓ Reading Check

What did the Chinese do to control flooding?

____

____

____

The Shang dynasty was the first civilization in China. It arose around 1760 B.C. The Shang people built China's first cities. They created some fine bronze work. The Shang also created the first Chinese alphabet.

About 600 years after the founding of the Shang dynasty, a new group emerged. The Zhou dynasty ruled lands that bordered Shang lands. They conquered the Shang and ruled from about 1122 B.C. Much later, there was a time known as the Warring States. Small kingdoms fought for control of ancient China.

The Chinese thought that rulers came to power because of fate. This idea was called the Mandate of Heaven. A mandate is a law. The Mandate of Heaven was used to support a king's right to rule his people. It also gave a father power over his family. ✓

Target Reading Skill

Which sentence states the main idea of the bracketed paragraph?

____

____

____

✓ Reading Check

What was the Mandate of Heaven?

____

____

____

Importance of the Family

The family was the center of early Chinese society. It was much more important than each person or the nation. The family came first.

A home in ancient China might contain up to five generations. A person's status in the **extended family** depended on age and sex. As a rule, the oldest man had the most rights and power. Women were expected to obey the men. When a woman married, she became part of her husband's family. ✓

The Chinese were the first people known to use two names. One was for the family and the other was for the person. In Chinese society, the family name comes first.

✓ Reading Check

What factors did a person's status depend on in early Chinese families?

1. ______________________________

2. ______________________________

Review Questions

1. What was the first known civilization in China?

____

____

2. Describe the importance of the family in early Chinese society.

____

____

____

Key Term

extended family (ek STEN did FAM uh lee) *n.* several generations of closely related people

Prepare to Read

Section 2 Confucius and His Teachings

Objectives

1. Learn about the life of Confucius.
2. Find out about the teachings of Confucius.
3. Understand the impact of Confucianism on Chinese society.

Identify Supporting Details The main idea of a paragraph or section is its most important point. The main idea is supported by details. Details give more information about the main idea. They may explain the main idea. They may give additional facts or examples. They tell you *what, where, why, how much,* or *how many.*

The main idea of the section titled "The Life of Confucius" is stated in this sentence: "Confucius was the most important early Chinese thinker."

As you read, notice how the details tell you more about the life of Confucius and why he was important.

Vocabulary Strategy

Recognizing Signal Words Signal words are words or phrases that give you clues. They help you understand what you read. They prepare you for what is coming next.

There are different kinds of signal words. Signal words may be used to sequence relationships. Sequence is the order in which things occur. It relates events in terms of when they happen.

Some signal words that may show sequence are:

first	*then*	*before*	*afterward*
next	*finally*	*earlier*	*later*

Section 2 Summary

The Life of Confucius

Confucius was the most important early Chinese thinker. The Chinese considered him to be a great teacher.

Confucius was born in 551 B.C. He came from a poor but noble family of the North China Plain. He loved learning and mostly taught himself. He hoped to get an important government office. He never succeeded. Instead, he decided to teach.

Confucius may have been China's first professional teacher. He charged students a fee to take classes. He taught his students his views of life and government. He was willing to teach poor students. But his students had to be very eager to learn. ✓

Later in his life, Confucius looked for a ruler who would follow his teachings. He could not find one. He died in 479 B.C. at the age of 73. He thought his life had been a failure. But his teachings would be followed in China for many centuries.

The Teachings of Confucius

Confucius was not an original thinker. Instead, he passed on the wise teachings of thinkers who lived before him. Many of his teachings were meant to make rulers reform. He wanted to bring peace, stability, and wealth to China.

Confucius' teachings make up a **philosophy** known as Confucianism. It was one of several philosophies in ancient China.

Confucius lived when there were many wars in China. Rulers wanted to get more power. They did not care about ruling wisely. Confucius hoped to persuade them to change their ways. His goal was to bring order to society. He thought there would be order if people behaved properly to each other. Society would prosper.

Key Terms

Confucius (kun FYOO shus) *n.* (551–479 B.C.) Chinese philosopher and teacher whose beliefs had a great influence on Chinese life
philosophy (fih LAHS uh fee) *n.* system of beliefs and values

✓ Reading Check

What kind of students did Confucius like to teach?

____

____

____

Target Reading Skill

Mark the Text

Underline the detail in the bracketed paragraph that supports the main idea that Confucius was an important Chinese thinker.

Confucius said that the people in power must set a good example. Confucianism is a philosophy, but also served as a religion for many people. It helped guide them. It told them how to behave. Some people practiced it alongside other religions.

There were many religions in ancient China. They included worship of ancestors and a belief in spirits. Most Chinese believed that they would be happy if they led a balanced life. These ideas were supported by Taoism (DOW iz um). Taoism followed the writings of Laozi (LOW dzuh). He was a Chinese thinker who lived in the 500s B.C. Taoists believe they should live simply. They should not be selfish. On the whole, Confucianism was more widely studied than Taoism. ✓

✓ Reading Check

Describe the religious traditions of ancient China.

____

____

____

The Influence of Confucius

Members of the Chinese **civil service** had to learn the teachings of Confucianism. Before Confucius, government posts were often given to the sons of important people. Afterward, they were based on merit. The men had to pass official tests. These tests were based on the teachings of Confucius.

Vocabulary Strategy

Look at the first three sentences in the bracketed paragraph. The events they describe are out of order. However, signal words show how the events are related to each other. List the events in the proper sequence.

1. ______________________________
2. ______________________________
3. ______________________________

The exams brought more able young men into government work. But candidates had to know how to read. This made it hard for a poor man to advance. But it was not impossible. ✓

✓ Reading Check

Why was it difficult for poor men to work in the civil service?

____

____

____

Review Questions

1. Why did Confucius think it was important to teach rulers how to behave?

____

____

____

2. How did the ideas of Confucius change the way civil servants were chosen in ancient China?

____

____

____

Key Term

civil service (SIV ul SUR vis) *n.* the group of people who carry out the work of the government

Prepare to Read

Section 3 Warring Kingdoms Unite

Objectives

1. Learn about the rise of the Qin dynasty.
2. Find out how Emperor Shi Huangdi tried to unify the economy and culture of China.
3. Look at the actions of the Han dynasty's leaders.

Target Reading Skill

Identify Implied Main Ideas The main idea of a paragraph or section is its most important point. Sometimes the main idea is not stated directly. Instead, all the details in a paragraph or section add up to a main idea. In this case, we say the main idea is implied. It is up to you to put the details together.

For example, let's say you are studying the details on the next page following the heading "The Qin Dynasty." You could then state the main idea this way: "China was unified and strengthened by its first emperor, Shi Huangdi."

Vocabulary Strategy

Recognizing Signal Words Signal words are words or phrases that give you clues. They help you understand what you read. They prepare you for what is coming next.

There are different kinds of signal words. Signal words may be used to show different kinds of relationships, such as contrast. Contrasts are the differences between things or ideas.

Some signal words that show contrast include:

but	*however*	*on the other hand*	*yet*
not	*despite*	*even though*	

Section 3 Summary

The Qin Dynasty

China's first emperor was **Shi Huangdi**. At first, he ruled the Qin (chin) people. They lived on China's western edge. By 221 B.C., he controlled most of the land that makes up modern-day China. His dynasty is called the Qin dynasty. The name China comes from "Ch'in," another way to spell *Qin*.

Target Reading Skill

State what all the details in the bracketed paragraph are about. Use only one sentence.

Shi Huangdi's rule was strong and harsh. For a long time, nomads had attacked the northern border of China. To stop this, Shi Huangdi ordered the largest building project in Chinese history. Earlier rulers had built walls to protect the border. He decided to link them. The wall took about ten years to build. It is now called the Great Wall of China. Later emperors repaired and added to the wall, making it even longer. ✓

✓ Reading Check

How was China's Great Wall built?

Shi Huangdi built roads to let his armies rush to the scene of any uprisings. He killed or imprisoned local rulers who opposed him. He divided all of China into districts run by his most trusted officials.

Unifying Economy and Culture

Shi Huangdi wanted his dynasty to have one culture and one economy. He ordered that one **currency** be used in China. This made it easier for one region of China to trade with another. He also said there should be a standard system of weights and measures. He ordered an improved system of writing and a law code.

In 213 B.C., Shi Huangdi outlawed Confucianism and other beliefs. He replaced them with the Qin philosophy of legalism. Legalism states that people should be punished for bad behavior and rewarded for good behavior. Legalists thought people should serve the emperor. Shi Huangdi burned almost all the books. Only books on medicine, technology, and farming were spared. When scholars protested, he killed them. ✓

✓ Reading Check

How did Shi Huangdi try to control his people's freedoms?

Shi Huangdi's empire did not last long after his death in 210 B.C. His dynasty lasted only 15 years.

Key Terms

Shi Huangdi (shur hwahng DEE) ***n.*** China's first emperor
currency (KUR un see) ***n.*** money used by a group or a nation

The Han Dynasty

Liu Bang helped defeat the Qin dynasty. By 202 B.C., he started the Han (hahn) dynasty. His government was stable. His rule was less harsh than Shi Huangdi's.

Stable governments were a mark of the Han dynasty. Han rulers wanted educated workers. They based the civil service system on Confucianism.

In 140 B.C. **Wudi** came to power. He was Liu Bang's great-grandson. He was about 15 years old. Wudi ruled for more than 50 years. He was mainly interested in war and the military. The Great Wall was improved. He made the army stronger and expanded China's land.

Wudi died in 87 B.C. China was still well-off under later Han emperors. Many new ideas and technologies were developed. But the empire was weaker. Several emperors were very young. Others fought for power. The empire began to fall apart.

As a result, **warlords** gained power. The last Han emperor was kept in power by a warlord. In A.D. 220, he replaced the Han dynasty with his own. This was the Wei dynasty. The Wei dynasty only controlled parts of northern China. It ended about 50 years later. China broke up into several smaller kingdoms. ✓

Vocabulary Strategy

Mark the Text

In the bracketed paragraph, a signal word is used to show contrast. Find the signal word and circle it. What is being contrasted here?

✓ Reading Check

What happened in A.D. 220?

Review Questions

1. What did Shi Huangdi do to unite the economy and culture of China?

2. What was government like in China under the Han dynasty?

Key Terms

Liu Bang (LYOH bahng) *n.* founder of the Han dynasty
Wudi (woo dee) *n.* Chinese emperor who brought the Han dynasty to its peak
warlord (WAWR lawrd) *n.* a local leader of an armed group

Prepare to Read

Section 4 Achievements of Ancient China

Objectives

1. Learn about the Silk Road.
2. Find out about the Han dynasty's respect for tradition and learning.
3. Discover what important advances in technology were made in China during the Han dynasty.

Target Reading Skill

Identify Supporting Details Each section of text has a main idea. The main idea is supported by details. The details give more information about the main idea.

On the next page, the main idea for the text under the heading "The Silk Road" is implied. It is not stated directly. But it can be determined by adding up the details and seeing what they are about. The main idea can be stated this way: "Both ideas and goods were exchanged along the Silk Road. It connected China to the Mediterranean."

As you read, note the supporting details under each heading.

Vocabulary Strategy

Recognizing Signal Words Signal words are words or phrases that give you clues. They prepare you for what is coming next.

There are different kinds of signal words. Signal words may show how things are related, such as cause and effect. As you will recall, a cause is what makes something happens. An effect is the result of the cause. Some signal words that may show cause and effect include:

Cause	Effect
because	*as a result*
if	*consequently*
on account of	*so*
since	*then*
	therefore

Section 4 Summary

The Silk Road

Wudi's conquests brought the Chinese into contact with the people of Central Asia. The Chinese exchanged goods with these people. A major trade route developed. It was called the **Silk Road**.

The Silk Road was a series of routes that covered more than 4,000 miles (6,400 kilometers). It crossed mountains and deserts. It ended in what is now Turkey. From there, traders shipped goods across the Mediterranean.

Few travelers went the entire length of the Silk Road. Instead, goods were passed from trader to trader as they crossed Asia. With each trade, the price went up. At the end, the goods were very expensive.

The Silk Road got its name from **silk**. Han farmers had developed new ways for raising silkworms, the caterpillars that made the silk. Wealthy Romans would pay high prices for Chinese silk. Wealthy Chinese would pay well for items from Rome. ✓

New ideas also traveled along the Silk Road. For example, missionaries from India traveled to China along the road. They brought Buddhism with them. By the end of the Han dynasty, Buddhism was a major religion in China.

Tradition and Learning

Tradition and learning flourished during the Han dynasty.

Tradition	Learning
• Rulers wanted to bring back respect for tradition • Returned to the teachings of Confucius • Civil service required study of Confucianism	• Poetry flourished • Scholars created first dictionary • Sima Qian wrote the a history of China ✓

Key Terms

Silk Road (silk rohd) *n.* an ancient trade route between China and Europe

silk (silk) *n.* a valuable cloth, made by silkworms

Target Reading Skill

The main idea of the section titled "The Silk Road" is "Both goods and ideas were exchanged along the Silk Road."

In the bracketed paragraphs find one example of each.

Goods: ____________________

Ideas: ____________________

✓ Reading Check

What are silkworms?

____

____

____

✓ Reading Check

What contribution to learning did Sima Qian make?

____

____

____

Vocabulary Strategy

In the bracketed paragraph, a signal word is used to show cause and effect. Find the signal word and circle it. Then write the cause and effect below.

Mark the Text

Cause: ______________________

____

Effect: ______________________

____

✓ Reading Check

What did the Chinese write on before they invented paper?

____

____

____

Han Technology

Because the Han government was stable, the Chinese worked on improving their society. At this time, China was the most advanced civilization in the world. Farming tools were improved. The Chinese invented many devices. These things did not reach Europe for many centuries.

The Chinese made advances in the arts, in bronze-working, building temples and palaces, and in jade carvings. They also made discoveries in the field of medicine. They learned about herbal remedies and accupunture. Besides improving farm tools, they also invented the compass and the rudder, a device used to steer ships.

One of the most important Chinese inventions was paper. At first, the Chinese used wood scrolls and bones to keep records. Later, they wrote messages and even whole books on silk. Then, around A.D. 105, they invented paper. Paper helped learning and the arts in China. After several centuries, the use of paper spread across Asia and into Europe. Paper replaced papyrus from Egypt as the material for scrolls and books. ✓

The Han dynasty ended in the A.D. 200s. But its deeds were not forgotten. People in China still call themselves "the children of Han."

Review Questions

1. How did the Silk Road get its name?

____

____

____

2. In what ways did the Han dynasty show a respect for Chinese traditions?

____

____

____

Key Term

Sima Qian (sih MAH chen) *n.* (c. 145–85 B.C.) a Chinese scholar who wrote the most important history of ancient China, *Historical Records*

Chapter 5 Assessment

1. The Chinese called the Huang River "China's Sorrow" because
   - **A.** it was so long.
   - **B.** it was the muddiest river in the world.
   - **C.** its floods could be very destructive.
   - **D.** its water was poisonous to both people and crops.

2. What is the Mandate of Heaven?
   - **A.** a Chinese religion based on the ideas of Confucius
   - **B.** the idea used to support a king's right to rule his people
   - **C.** the belief that soldiers killed in battle will go directly to heaven
   - **D.** none of the above

3. The main goal of Confucianism was to
   - **A.** serve as a religion that would unify the people of China.
   - **B.** live in harmony with nature.
   - **C.** provide training for members of the Chinese civil service.
   - **D.** bring order to society.

4. How did Shi Huangdi try to control people's thoughts?
   - **A.** He replaced Confucianism with legalism.
   - **B.** He ordered books to be burned.
   - **C.** He had scholars killed when they protested.
   - **D.** all of the above

5. During which dynasty was paper invented?
   - **A.** the Shang dynasty
   - **B.** the Zhou dynasty
   - **C.** the Qin dynasty
   - **D.** the Han dynasty

Short Answer Question

Why was the Silk Road important?

____

____

____

____

____

Prepare to Read

Section 1
Early Greek Civilization

Objectives

1. Find out about the geography of Greece.
2. Learn about the rise of civilization in ancient Greece
3. Study the start of government in ancient Greece.

Target Reading Skill

Use Word Parts Often, when you come across an unfamiliar word, you can break the word into parts. This can help you recognize and pronounce it. You may find roots, prefixes, or suffixes.

A root is the base of the word. A suffix is attached to the end of a root. It changes the word's meaning. It may change the word's part of speech. For example, adding a suffix may change a verb into a noun. Verbs are words that show action. They tell what someone or something is doing. Nouns are words that name things.

In this section, you will read the word *fortification*. The suffix *-ion* makes the word a noun. If you know the meaning of the word *fortify*, you can figure out *fortification*. Break the word into a root and suffix to learn its meaning.

Vocabulary Strategy

Using Word Origins Many English words come from ancient Greek. Often, words of Greek origin have more than one root. Also, a Greek word can be the root of more than one English word.

Look at the words *aristocracy* and *democracy*. Each of these words is made up of two Greek roots:

aristos ("best") + *kratia* ("rule") = *aristocracy* ("rule [or government] by the best")

demos ("people") + *kratia* ("rule") = *democracy* ("rule [or government] by the people")

Other English words that use these Greek roots include *aristocrat*, *aristocratic*, *democrat*, *democratic*, *autocracy*, and *theocracy*.

Section 1 Summary

The Geography of Greece

Greece is a land made up of **peninsulas** and small islands. Mountains are the major landform. Only about one fifth of Greece is good for growing crops. No wonder the Greeks became traders and sailors!

In a way, the ancient Greeks were all islanders. Some lived on real islands. Others lived in communities separated from each other by mountains. Each community developed its own customs and beliefs. The Greeks often fought among themselves. But they had the same heritage, language, and gods. ✓

The Rise of Greek Civilization

From about 3000 to about 1100 B.C., the Minoans (mih NOH unz) lived on the island of Crete. They were sea traders. In the middle of the 1400s B.C., their civilization declined.

The Mycenaeans (my suh NEE unz) lived on the mainland. They were at the height of their power around 1400 B.C. The Mycenaeans spoke an early form of modern Greek. They spread their power through conquest.

Greek myth tells the story of the Trojan War. Two long poems, the *Iliad* and the *Odyssey,* tell of a struggle between Greece and the city of Troy. The poet Homer is given credit for them. The poems taught the Greeks how their noblest heroes behaved.

After the Trojan War, Greek civilization fell apart. No one knows why. People were very poor. They forgot the art of writing. These years have been called Greece's Dark Ages. They lasted from the early 1100s B.C. to about 750 B.C. During this time, people resettled near hills. They built fortifications to protect them from attack. Such a fortified hill was called an **acropolis**. ✓

Key Terms

peninsula (puh NIN suh luh) *n.* an area of land almost completely surrounded by water and connected to the mainland by a narrow strip of land
acropolis (uh KRAH puh lis) *n.* the fortified hill of an ancient Greek city

✓ Reading Check

What do we mean when we say the ancient Greeks were all islanders?

____

____

____

Target Reading Skill

If *fortify* means "strengthen," what does *fortification* in the paragraph below, mean?

____

____

____

✓ Reading Check

What happened in Greece's Dark Ages?

____

____

____

Vocabulary Strategy

If *aristocracy* is "government by the best," what would an *aristocrat* be?

____

____

____

✓ Reading Check

What were the three requirements one needed to be a citizen in Athens?

1. ______________________
2. ______________________
3. ______________________

Governing Ancient Greece

Around 750 B.C., city-states began to form. Each one formed near an acropolis. Each was more or less independent. The early rulers were probably chieftains or kings. By the end of the Dark Ages, most city-states were ruled by **aristocrats**. They controlled most of the land. They could afford the best weapons.

The city-states became richer through trade. A middle class formed. It was made up of merchants and artisans. They became more powerful than the aristocrats. New rulers took over the government. They were called **tyrants**. They were supported by the middle classes.

Some tyrants were too harsh. These were overthrown. Some of the cities adopted a form of government called **democracy**. One of them was Athens. In the 500s B.C., Athens gave male citizens who were at least 18 a say in government.

Only about one in five Athenians was a citizen. Only men could be citizens. A citizen had to have two parents who came from families with citizenship. ✓

Review Questions

1. Describe the geography of ancient Greece.

____

____

2. What were the three kinds of government that developed in the Greek city-states after the Dark Ages?

____

____

Key Terms

aristocrat (uh RIS tuh krat) *n.* a member of a rich and powerful family
tyrant (TY runt) *n.* a ruler who takes power by force
democracy (dih MAHK ruh see) *n.* a form of government in which citizens govern themselves

Prepare to Read

Section 2 Religion, Philosophy, and the Arts

Objectives

1. Discover what characterized the Golden Age of Athens.
2. Learn about the religious beliefs of the ancient Greeks.
3. Find out about science, philosophy, and the arts in ancient Greece.

Target Reading Skill

Use Word Parts When you see an unfamiliar word, try to break the word into parts. This will help you recognize and pronounce it. You may find roots, prefixes, or suffixes. Look back to Chapter 3 of this workbook to review finding roots, and Chapter 4 to review using prefixes and suffixes.

A prefix goes in front of the word. It changes the meaning of the word. In this section you will read the word *dishonoring*. Break the word into a prefix and a root to learn its meaning. (The prefix *dis-* means *away from* or *the opposite of*.)

Vocabulary Strategy

Using Word Origins Many English words come from ancient Greek. Most of the Greek words that are used in English are spelled differently. As you read this chapter, you will come across many words of Greek origin.

The Greeks used sports and plays to honor their gods at religious feasts. Many words used to describe both sports and theater have Greek origins. Some of them are listed in the table below.

Greek Words	English Words
diskos	discus
drama	drama
choros	chorus
komoidia	comedy
tragoidia	tragedy

These words also serve as the base for many other English words, including *dramatic*, *choral*, *comic*, *comedian*, and *tragic*.

✓ Reading Check

How did Pericles strengthen democracy?

____

____

____

Vocabulary Strategy

The modern Olympic games are based on games that were held every four years to honor Zeus. They were held at Mt. Olympus. How do you think the Olympic games got their name?

____

____

____

✓ Reading Check

Circle the ways the Greeks honored their gods.

✓ Reading Check

Which three important philosophers taught in Athens?

1. ______________________________
2. ______________________________
3. ______________________________

Section 2 Summary

The Golden Age of Athens

The Golden Age of Athens was from 479 to 431 B.C. During that time, philosophy and the arts did well. Democracy was at its peak. Athens grew rich from trade and from silver mined by slaves. Its allies paid **tribute**. This added to the city's wealth.

For about 30 years, the most powerful man in politics was Pericles (PEHR uh kleez). He was an aristocrat. However, he began reforms to make democracy stronger. One reform required that the city pay a salary to its officials. This meant that poor citizens could hold office. ✓

Religious Beliefs in Ancient Greece

The Greek gods had human forms They also had many human characteristics. There were 12 great gods led by Zeus. Zeus ruled gods and men. He lived on Greece's highest mountain, Mt. Olympus. The Greeks also honored less important gods and mythical heroes.

Each city-state honored one of the 12 great gods. They built a temple to that god. Every four years, there was an Olympic festival. They held games to honor Zeus. Modern Olympic games are based on this. ✓

The Greeks visited **oracles**. There they asked the gods for advice. Answers were given by a priest or priestess. Heads of state often sought advice on governing. The oracles had a great impact on Greek history.

Greek Science and Philosophy

In the Golden Age and later on, important **philosophers** taught in Athens. The ideas of three men influenced thinking for a long time. They were Socrates (SAHK ruh teez), Plato (PLAY toh), and Aristotle (AIR uh staht ul). ✓

Key Terms

tribute (TRIB yoot) *n.* regular payment made to a powerful state or nation by a weaker one
oracle (AWR uh kul) *n.* in ancient Greece, a sacred site where a god or goddess was consulted
philosopher (fih LAHS uh fur) *n.* someone who uses reason to understand the world

Philosophers	Life and Beliefs
Socrates	Asked questions that scared people Put on trial for dishonoring the gods Sentenced to death
Plato	Student of Socrates Distrusted democracy because of what happened to Socrates Believed society should have workers, soldiers, and philosopher-rulers
Aristotle	Student of Plato Thought people should use reason to gain knowledge

Visual and Dramatic Arts

The Greeks used architecture and sculpture to honor their gods. The Acropolis was the religious heart of Athens. It had been destroyed in 480 B.C. in a war. Pericles rebuilt it to glorify the city.

With the new Acropolis, Greek architecture reached its peak. The greatest building was a temple to the goddess Athena. The building is called the Parthenon. The Parthenon was filled with beautiful, lifelike sculptures.

Athenians were the first people to write dramas, or plays. Some of the most famous Greek plays were **tragedies**. Between scenes, a chorus sang poems. In most plays, the chorus gave background information or praised the gods. Tragedies were performed for religious feasts. Comedies were also presented. They made fun of well-known citizens and customs of the day. ✓

Review Questions

1. What was the Golden Age of Athens?

2. What kinds of visual and dramatic art did Greeks create?

Key Term

tragedy (TRAJ uh dee) *n.* a type of serious drama that usually ends in disaster for the main character

Target Reading Skill

Find the underlined word in the table. If *dis-* means "taking away from" or "the opposite of," what do you think *dishonoring* means?

✓ Reading Check

What was the role of the chorus in Greek drama?

Prepare to Read

Section 3 Daily Life in Athens

Objectives

1. Learn about public life in Athens.
2. Find out how the people of Athens spent their time at home.
3. Learn about slavery and its effects in ancient Greece.

Target Reading Skill

Recognize Word Origins The origin of a word is where the word comes from. The English language is full of words from other languages, such as Greek, Latin, and German. Some of these words are used in their original form. Often, they have changed over time. Sometimes, a foreign word or root is joined with English prefixes or suffixes. The two together then make a new word.

In this section, you will read the word *splendor*. It comes from the Latin word *splendere*, which means "to shine." In *splendor*, the suffix *-or* means "quality." Use your knowledge of the origin of *splendor* and the context to figure out what *splendor* means.

There are other English words that come from *splendere*. One of them is *splendid*, which means "having splendor." Another is *resplendent*, which means "full of splendor."

Vocabulary Strategy

Using Word Origins Many English words come from ancient Greek. Often, words of Greek origin combine more than one root. The same roots may be used in a number of combinations. Often a Greek word is the root of many other words in English.

The Greek word *agora* appears in the English word *agoraphobia*. *Agora* means "open place" or "open area." The word *phobia* is also from Greek. It means "abnormal fear or dread." Thus, agoraphobia is an abnormal fear of being in open places.

The word *acropolis* is made up of two Greek roots, *akros* ("top" or "high") and *polis* ("city"). Other English words that contain one of these roots include *acrobat*, *acrophobia*, and *metropolis*.

Section 3 Summary

Life in Public

Each Greek city had an **agora**. The one in **Athens** was the busiest and most interesting. The Acropolis rose in splendor above it. The Acropolis was the hub of religious life in Athens. But the Agora was the hub of public life.

In the morning, many Athenian men went to the Agora. They talked of politics and philosophy. Sometimes they just gossiped. Around them, buyers and **vendors** bargained for good prices. The streets were lined with shops. Farmers and artisans sold their wares from stands. Foods and other goods were sold there. Temples and government buildings lined the Agora. ✓

At Home in Athens

Throughout Greece, private homes were plain. Most were built of mud bricks. Rooms were set around an open courtyard that was hidden from the street. The courtyard was the center of the household. Rooms might include a kitchen, storerooms, a dining room, and bedrooms. Water had to be carried from a public fountain.

The ancient Greeks ate simple foods. Breakfast might be just bread. Midday meals might add cheese or olives to the bread. Dinner would be a hot meal. It might consist of fish and vegetables. These might be followed by cheese, fruit, and cakes. Most Athenians ate little meat. ✓

Most of the people in the Agora were men. Athenian women spent their days at home. They had little freedom. They could not take part in politics or vote. They could not own property. However, they could be priestesses in religious groups.

Key Terms

agora (AG uh ruh) *n.* a public market and meeting place
Athens (ATH unz) *n.* a city-state in ancient Greece; the capital of modern-day Greece
vendor (VEN dur) *n.* a seller of goods

Target Reading Skill

Combine your knowledge of the Latin word *splendere* and the suffix *-or* with the context to figure out the meaning of *splendor*.

____

____

____

✓ Reading Check

What business did Athenians conduct in the Agora?

____

____

____

✓ Reading Check

What kinds of foods did Athenians eat?

____

____

____

Women ran the home and family. Women did spinning and weaving. They looked after food and wine supplies. They cared for young children. They also kept track of family finances. If a family had slaves, they were also the woman's responsibility. She gave them their orders and trained them. She also cared for them when they were sick.

Slavery in Ancient Greece

Slavery was common throughout Greece. Historians say that as many as 100,000 slaves may have lived in Athens. That is almost one third of the population. Many free people were enslaved when they were captured during war. Others were captured by pirates while traveling on ships. Some slaves were the children of slaves. Many slaves were foreigners. Some Greeks did not want to own other Greeks. ✓

Slaves did many kinds of work. Some worked on farms. Others worked in the mines. Still others assisted artisans. Most Greek households could not run without slaves. Slaves cooked, served food, tended children, and wove cloth. Household slaves were often treated like members of the family. Slaves who worked in mines suffered the most. Their work was not only tiring, but also dangerous. The work of slaves allowed the free citizens of Athens time to pursue art, philosophy, and public service.

✓ Reading Check

Why were many slaves in Greece foreigners?

____

____

____

Vocabulary Strategy

Philosophy comes from Greek words for "love" (*philos*) and "wisdom" (*sophia*). Based on this information, what do you think *philosophy* means?

____

____

____

Review Questions

1. What activities took place in the Agora of Athens?

____

____

____

2. Describe the roles of slaves in ancient Greece.

____

____

____

Key Term

slavery (SLAY vur ee) *n.* condition of being owned by someone else

Prepare to Read

Section 4 Sparta and Athens

Objectives

1. Find out what it was like to live in the ancient city of Sparta.
2. Learn about the Persian invasion of Greece.
3. Examine conflicts faced by the Athenian Empire.

Target Reading Skill

Recognize Word Origins In this section, you will read the word *rebellion.* It contains the Latin root *-belli-*, which means "war." The suffix *-ion* means "the act of." Consider how the word is used in its context. What do you think *rebellion* means?

The word *rebellion* is a noun. A noun is a word that names a thing or idea. We can change the word to an adjective by changing the suffix. The suffix *–ious* means like, or full of. Then the word becomes *rebellious.* Do you think the word *rebellious* means something different than the word *rebellion*?

The word *rebel* is related to *rebellion* and *rebellious.* Other words with the same root include *belligerent* and *bellicose.*

Vocabulary Strategy

Using Word Origins As you read this chapter, you will come across many words of Greek origin.

Some English words are based on Greek words that were originally the names of people or places. The table below lists a few of them.

Greek Name	English Word	Meaning
Marathon	marathon	a long-distance foot race
Olympus	Olympic	relating to the modern Olympic games
Solon	solon	a lawmaker, especially a wise one
Sparta	Spartan	like the Spartans; plain

Section 4 Summary

Living in Sparta

Life in **Sparta** was the opposite of life in Athens. It was harsh. The Spartans were tough and grim. Sparta's army equaled Athens' in the 400s B.C. But Sparta never matched Athens' other achievements.

In its early days, Sparta was much like other Greek cities. In the 600s B.C., there were wars in and around the city. The wars turned Sparta into a strong war machine. There was one basic rule: Always put the city's needs above your own.

Early on, the Spartans conquered the land around their city. They turned the conquered people into **helots**. Helots did all the farm work on land owned by Spartan citizens. This left the Spartans free to wage war. There were far more helots than Spartans. Fearing a <u>rebellion</u>, the Spartans turned their city into an armed camp.

The government controlled the life of each Spartan from an early age. Military training began at age seven for boys. It went on for 13 years. Boys were taught to endure pain, hardship, and punishment in silence.

Girls also trained and competed in wrestling and spear throwing. They were not expected to become soldiers. But Spartans believed that strong, healthy girls would have strong, healthy children. Spartan women had more freedom than women in other Greek city-states. They were allowed to own land. They even took some part in business. ✓

The Persians Invade

Much of Greek history tells of wars they fought with each other. But in the 400s B.C., Persia posed a new threat.

In 490 B.C., thousands of Persians landed in Greece itself. They grouped at <u>Marathon</u>. It was about 26 miles (40 kilometers) north of Athens. There were twice as many Persians as Athenians. After a few days, the

Key Terms

Sparta (SPAHR tuh) *n.* a city-state in ancient Greece
helot (HEL ut) *n.* servants in ancient Sparta

Target Reading Skill

Find the underlined word in the third paragraph to the right. Use what you know about the Latin root *-belli-*, to find the meaning of *rebellion*. *Hint:* Look for context clues.

✓ Reading Check

What was life like for the women of Sparta?

Vocabulary Strategy

In ancient Greece *Marathon* was a place. Today the word has a very different meaning. From the facts that follow see if you can figure out how *marathon* got its new meaning. The Greeks wanted to warn the city of Athens that the Persians were a short distance away. So one soldier ran the entire 26 miles to warn the city.

What does *marathon* mean today?

Athenians rushed the Persians with no warning. The Persians were beaten. One account says that the Athenians killed about 6,400 Persians. They lost only 192 soldiers themselves. ✓

More battles followed. The Greeks united for a short time to drive off the Persians.

Conflict and the Athenian Empire

After the Persians were beaten, the power of Athens spread through much of eastern Greece. Athens became partners with other city-states.

In time, Athens began to treat the other city-states unfairly. These city-states paid Athens money to protect them. Athens used the money for new buildings. Some of these city-states began to look to Sparta to protect them. In 431 B.C., fighting began between allies of Sparta and Athens. The war went on for 27 years. It was called the **Peloponnesian War**. The war was named for Pelopponese, the southern Greek peninsula where Sparta was located.

Early in the war, Athens was struck by a **plague**. It killed about one third of the people. Pericles died in the plague. In 405 B.C., the Spartans set up a **blockade**. They closed the harbor so Athens could not get food. The Athenians gave up in 404 B.C. The Athenians never again controlled the ancient Greek world. ✓

Review Questions

1. Describe what life was like for people living in Sparta.

____

____

2. How did the Greeks beat the Persians who invaded them?

____

____

Key Terms

Peloponnesian War (pel uh puh NEE shun wawr) *n.* (431–404 B.C.), war fought between Athens and Sparta in ancient Greece
plague (playg) *n.* a widespread disease
blockade (blah KAYD) *n.* an action taken to isolate the enemy

✓ Reading Check

What happened during the battle at Marathon?

____

____

____

✓ Reading Check

How did the Spartans finally defeat the Athenians?

____

____

____

Prepare to Read

Section 5 The Spread of Greek Culture

1. Learn how Alexander the Great built his empire.
2. Find out about the age of Hellenism, when Greek culture spread to other parts of the world.

Target Reading Skill

Use Word Parts When you come across an unfamiliar word, break the word into parts. This will help you recognize it and pronounce it.

In this section you will read the word *extensive.* Break it into a prefix, root, and suffix to figure out its meaning. The prefix *ex-* means "out." The Latin root *-ten-* means "stretch." The suffix *-ive* means "relating to." It also changes the word to an adjective. An adjective is a word that describes something.

Some other words that are related to *extensive* include *extend* and *extent. Extend* is a verb. A verb is a word that shows action. *Extent* is a noun. A noun is a word that names a thing or an idea.

Vocabulary Strategy

Using Word Origins Many English words come from ancient Greek. Often, words of Greek origin combine more than one root. The same roots may be used in a number of different combinations. Often a Greek word is the root of many other words in English.

Many words dealing with science and math are of Greek origin, or have Greek roots. You can see this from the following list:

geo ("earth") + *metria* ("measurement") = *geometry*

geo ("earth") + *graphos* ("writing") = *geography*

geo ("earth") + *logos* ("word" or "science") = *geology*

bio ("life") + *logos* ("word" or "science") = *biology*

physike ("nature") = *physics*

mathematikos ("mathematical") = *mathematics*

Section 5 Summary

King Philip of Macedonia (mas uh DOH nee uh) hired the Greek philosopher Aristotle to teach his son Alexander. Macedonia was just north of Greece. Alexander thought he was Greek. But people in Athens did not think the Macedonians were Greeks. They thought the Macedonians were **barbarians**.

Alexander's Empire

King Philip united Macedonia. He built an army that was stronger than Sparta's. He captured many Greek city-states. He planned to attack Persia. But in 336 B.C. he was **assassinated**. At age 20, his son Alexander became king. He is known as **Alexander the Great**. ✓

One of the first things Alexander did was to invade the Persian Empire. In 11 years, he had conquered an extensive area. Persia and Egypt were part of his lands. Wherever Alexander went, he built cities. He gave many of them his own name.

Alexander's army was tired from years of fighting. Not far beyond the Indus River, his troops refused to go any farther. Alexander turned back. In Babylon, he came down with a fever. In 323 B.C., he died. It was only 13 years since he had come to the throne. But his conquests brought Greek culture to a vast area.

The Hellenistic Age

Within 50 years, Alexander's empire had broken up. There were three main kingdoms left. But, Greek culture was still alive in these **Hellenistic** kingdoms. (*Hellenistic* comes from the word *Hellas*, the name Greeks gave their land.)

Key Terms

barbarian (bar BEHR ee un) *n.* a wild and uncivilized person
assassinate (uh SAS uh nayt) *v.* to murder for political reasons
Alexander the Great (al ig ZAN dur thuh grayt) *n.* king of Macedonia from 336–323 B.C.; conqueror of Persia and Egypt and invader of India
Hellenistic (hel uh NIS tik) *adj.* describing Greek history or culture after the death of Alexander the Great, including the three main kingdoms formed by the breakup of Alexander's empire

✓ Reading Check

What event caused Alexander to become king?

____

____

____

Target Reading Skill

Use word parts to figure out what *extensive* means. Does your definition make sense in this paragraph?

Definition: ______________________

____

____

____

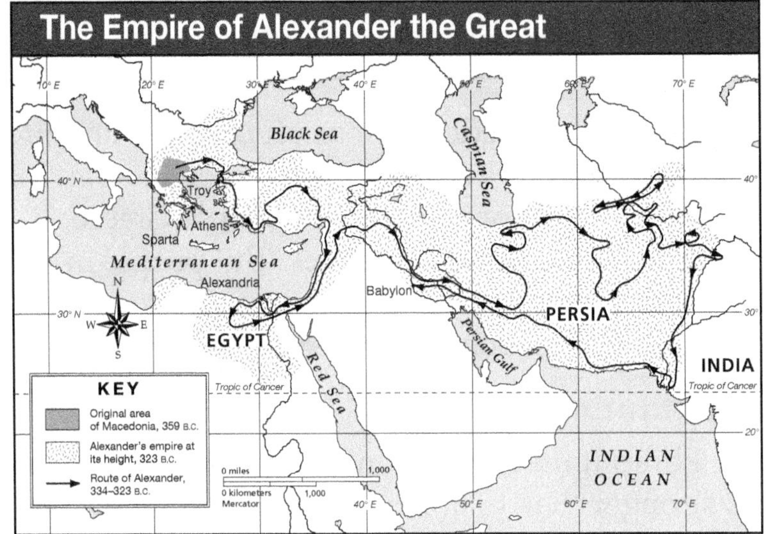

Alexander tried not to destroy the cultures of those he beat in war. He hoped that their culture would mix with Greek culture. This did not happen in the three Hellenistic kingdoms. Their cities were like Greek cities. Greek kings ruled. Greeks held the best jobs.

The greatest Hellenistic city was Alexandria, Egypt. It was founded in 332 B.C. at the edge of the Nile Delta. It became the capital of Egypt. Alexandria was the learning center of the Greek world. It had the largest library in the world. Scholars from many lands came to use its huge collection. ✓

Math and science also did well in Alexandria. Around 300 B.C., a mathematician named Euclid (YOO klid) developed geometry. Geometry is the branch of math that deals with figures such as angles, squares and cubes. Mathematicians today still use his system.

In Hellenistic times, many scholars knew Earth was round. A scholar named Eratosthenes (ehr uh TAHS thuh neez) figured out the distance around Earth.

✓ Reading Check

Why did many scholars go to Alexandria?

____

____

____

Vocabulary Strategy

If you know that "geo" means "earth" and "metria" means "measurement" what do you think *geometry* means?

____

____

____

Review Questions

1. How did Alexander's upbringing affect his attitude toward Greek culture?

____

____

2. Why was Alexandria, Egypt important?

____

____

Chapter 6 Assessment

1. Why did ancient Greek communities think they were separate countries?
   A. They spoke different languages.
   B. They had different gods.
   C. They were originally from different parts of the world.
   D. They were separated from each other by geography.

2. Who was the most powerful man in Athenian politics during the Golden Age?
   A. Aristotle
   B. Pericles
   C. Plato
   D. Socrates

3. Most of the labor in ancient Athenian households was done by
   A. women.
   B. children.
   C. slaves.
   D. helots.

4. What were the Spartans well known for?
   A. being the first people to write dramas
   B. their war skills
   C. their art
   D. philosophy and science

5. Which of the following is NOT true of the three Hellenistic kingdoms?
   A. They were ruled by Alexander the Great.
   B. Their cities were Greek cities.
   C. Greeks held the best jobs .
   D. Greek kings ruled.

Short Answer Question

How did Athens lose control over the rest of Greece?

____

____

____

____

____

Prepare to Read

Section 1
The Roman Republic

Objectives

1. Find out about the geography and early settlement of Rome.
2. Examine features of the Roman Republic and why it was founded.
3. Learn about the decline of the Roman Republic.

Identify Sequence A sequence is the order in which a group of events occurs. As you read, study the sequence of important events. To help track events, make a chart like the one below. The first event is filled in for you. Fill in the event that happens next when you come across it as you read. The arrows show how one event leads to the next.

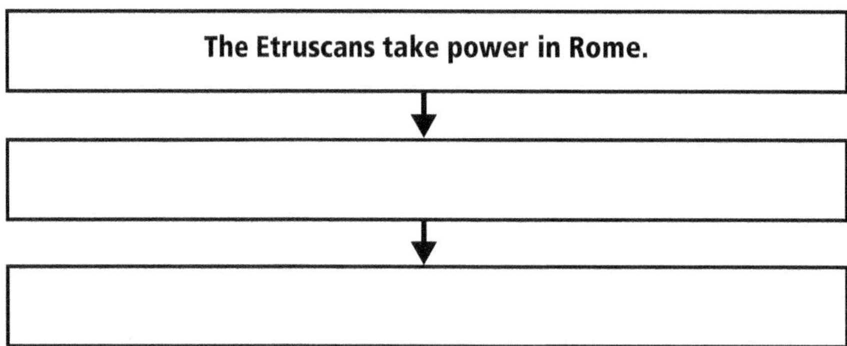

Vocabulary Strategy

Using Word Origins Many English words come from Latin. Latin was once a very popular language in Rome and other places. Most of the Latin words that are used in English are spelled differently. The meanings may be different too. As you read this chapter, you will read many words that came from Latin.

Below are words from Latin that have something to do with government. The original Latin word is in parentheses after the English word.

republic (res publica), senate (senatus), consul (consulere),
veto (vetare), justice (justitia), emperor (imperator)

Section 1 Summary

Rome's Geography

People first settled in Rome because it was a good place to live. The Tiber River flowed through it. The soil was fertile. Rome's seven hills made it easy to defend. Rome was at the center of the peninsula now called Italy, at the center of the known world.

The first settlements date from the 900s B.C. About 600 B.C., the Etruscans (ih TRUS kunz) took power. In 509 B.C., the Romans drove out the Etruscans. The Romans got many of their gods from the Etruscans. They also copied the Greek alphabet, which the Etruscans used, and the toga. ✓

Romans Form a Republic

The Romans did not want to rely on one ruler. They created a form of government called a **republic**. The leaders rule in the name of the people. The government was led by two **consuls**. But its most powerful part was the senate. It advised the consuls on foreign affairs, laws, finances, and other things. The consuls almost always took the senate's advice.

At first, the senate was made up of 300 **patricians** or upper-class people. The consuls were also patricians. Poorer citizens were called **plebeians**. For years, they could not hold office. Then, in 367 B.C. a law said at least one consul had to be a plebeian. Plebeians could also be senators.

There were limits to the power of the two consuls. They ruled for one year only. Both had to agree before the government could take any action. Either consul could **veto** an action. If the consuls disagreed in an emergency, a **dictator** could be appointed for six months.

Key Terms

republic (rih PUB lik) *n.* a government in which citizens select their leaders
consul (KAHN sul) *n.* a leader of the Roman Republic
patrician (puh TRISH un) *n.* a member of an upper-class family
plebeian (plih BEE un) *n.* an ordinary citizen
veto (VEE toh) *n.* the rejection of any planned action or rule by a person in power
dictator (DIK tay tur) *n.* a ruler who has total control

✓ Reading Check

What is known about the Etruscans?

____

____

____

Vocabulary Strategy

The word *government* comes from the Latin word *gubernare* (to guide [a ship]) and the suffix *-ment* (a way of). Based on this, what do you think *government* means?

____

____

____

Target Reading Skill

Read the bracketed paragraph. List the sequence of events that led to jobless plebeians moving to the city.

First: ______________________

____

Second: ______________________

____

Third: ______________________

____

Within about 250 years, Rome had conquered most of Italy. The patricians grew wealthy from the riches of the defeated people. They created large farms from land they bought from small farmers. Patricians used slaves to work the farms. As a result, many plebeian farmers found themselves without work. Jobless plebeians moved to the city. ✓

Angry plebeians decided they would not fight in the Roman army. Only then did the patricians give in to one of the demands of the plebeians. They set up a written code of laws called the Laws of the Twelve Tables. It applied equally to all citizens.

Meanwhile, Roman armies invaded Carthage, in North Africa. Next they conquered Spain and Greece. They then looked toward Gaul, which is now France.

✓ Reading Check

What complaints did the plebeians have against the patricians?

____

____

____

The Decline of the Republic

By 120 B.C., Rome was in trouble. For the next 75 years, generals with their own armies fought for power. Rome was about to break up. Then a new leader, Julius Caesar, came along.

Caesar was eager for power. War broke out between Caesar and the senate. Caesar won and became dictator in 48 B.C. Four years later he became dictator for life. Many senators hated the idea that Rome seemed to have a king. On March 15, 44 B.C., Caesar was assassinated by a group of senators.

Thirteen years of civil war followed. At the end, Caesar's adopted son, Octavian, held power. In 27 B.C., the senate gave him the title Augustus. It means "highly respected." He was the first emperor of Rome. The Roman Republic had lasted nearly 500 years. ✓

✓ Reading Check

What events followed the death of Caesar?

____

____

____

Review Questions

1. Describe the geography and early settlement of Rome.

____

____

2. What were the important features of the Roman Republic?

____

____

Prepare to Read

Section 2 The Roman Empire

Objectives

1. Learn about the rule of the Roman Empire and the empire's conquered peoples.
2. Look at the influence of Greece on Rome.
3. Find out about Roman advances in architecture, technology, and science.
4. Learn about the laws of Rome.

Target Reading Skill

Recognize Signal Words Signal words are words or phrases that prepare you for what is coming next. They are like road signs that tell drivers when to exit or how far the next town is.

Some important signal words tell about the sequence of events. Some common signal words include *when, first, before, during this time, after,* and *in* (followed by a date). They signal the order in which events took place. This section talks about the Roman Empire. To help keep the order of events clear as you read, look for signal words and phrases.

Vocabulary Strategy

Using Word Origins Almost half of the words in English used to be Latin words. Sometimes the spelling of the word or word's meaning has changed over time.

The word *republic* is an English word that comes from the Latin *res publica.* Look for the word *public* in both words. A republic is a government in which citizens who have the right to vote select their leaders. Public means "of the people." Other English words that are related to this idea include *publication, published,* and *publicity.*

Section 2 Summary

Ruling an Empire

Under the rule of Augustus and other emperors who followed, Rome added territory to the empire. The **Pax Romana** began with Augustus. It lasted for about 200 years. Augustus was a smart ruler. He often ignored the senate. But he did not act like a king.

The Romans treated the people they conquered wisely. The Romans did not force their way of life on those they conquered. The Romans wanted peaceful **provinces** that would provide raw materials, buy Roman goods, and pay taxes. Many of the conquered people took on Roman ways.

Augustus died in A.D. 14. For the next 82 years, there were good, bad, and terrible emperors. In A.D. 96, Rome entered the age of the "five good emperors." Perhaps the best of them was Hadrian (HAY dree un). He issued a code of laws, he reorganized the army, and he encouraged learning. The last of the "good emperors" was Marcus Aurelius (aw REE lee us). ✓

Circle the words and phrases in the bracketed paragraph that signal sequence

Why was Hadrian considered to be one of the "five good emperors"?

___

___

___

The Greek Influence on Rome

The Romans admired what the Greeks had achieved. Many Romans studied Greek art, architecture, and ideas about government. Greek religion had an effect on Roman religion. Many Roman gods and goddesses were similar to Greek gods and goddesses.

The Greeks and Romans both loved to learn, but liked different subjects. The Greeks cared about truth and ideas. The Romans used Greek ideas to build things. They became skilled architects and engineers. ✓

✓ Reading Check

What did the Greeks and Romans study?

___

___

___

Architecture and Technology

At first, Roman art and architecture looked like the Etruscans'. Later, the Romans copied Greek art and architecture. Then they developed their own style.

Key Terms

Pax Romana (paks roh MAH nah) *n.* the period of stability and prosperity in the Roman Empire, lasting from 27 B.C. to A.D. 180; "Roman peace"
province (PRAH vins) *n.* a part of an empire; area of the Roman Empire ruled by a governor, who was supported by an army

Roman statues and buildings were heavier and stronger than those of the Greeks. The Romans used arches to build larger structures. Most large buildings were made of bricks covered with thin slabs of marble. The Romans used concrete to put up the first tall buildings. The **Colosseum** was possibly the greatest Roman building. It was so big it held 50,000 people. ✓

Roman engineers built roads that went all over the empire. The Romans were famous for their **aqueducts**. They were miles and miles of arches. A channel along the top carried water from the countryside to the cities.

Roman Law

Roman law, like Roman roads, spread throughout the empire. The ruler Justinian (juh STIN ee uhn) used Roman law to create a famous code of justice. The code included a law to protect people from being forced out of their homes, and a law that did not allow people to be punished for expressing an opinion. ✓

Roman law has passed down to other cultures, including our own. Other Roman ideas of justice can also be seen in our own system. For example, people in Rome accused of crimes had the right to face their accusers. If there was doubt about a person's guilt, he or she would be judged innocent.

Review Questions

1. How did Rome solve the problems of governing its large empire?

____

____

____

2. What did the Romans learn from the Greeks?

____

____

____

Key Terms

Colosseum (kahl uh SEE um) *n.* a large amphitheater built in Rome around A.D. 70; site of contests and combats between people and animals

aqueduct (AK wuh dukt) *n.* a structure that carries water over long distances

✓ Reading Check

Mark the Text

Underline some of the details that describe a Roman building.

Vocabulary Strategy

The English word *channel* comes from the Latin word *canalis*. Look at the first five letters of *canalis*. What English word do you see?

____

____

____

✓ Reading Check

What are two laws from Justinian's Code?

1. ______________________________

____

2. ______________________________

____

Prepare to Read

Section 3 Roman Daily Life

Objectives

1. Learn about the social classes of ancient Rome.
2. Find out what family life looked like in ancient Rome.
3. Examine slavery in Rome.

Target Reading Skill

Recognize Sequence Signal Words You use sequence signal words all the time. Let's say you wanted to tell a friend about your vacation. You would use words such as *first, and then, but before that.* Those words tell your friend the order of events of your vacation. It's the same when you read. Signal words are words or phrases that give you clues. They help you understand what you are reading.

One of the most common uses of signal words is to show the passing of time. Signal words can also link together ideas or events.

This section looks at daily life and customs in ancient Rome. Ways of life in Rome changed over time. As you read, look for words and phrases that signal time such as *over time, later, today,* and *next.*

Vocabulary Strategy

Using Word Origins Some of the Latin words that are used in English have somewhat different meanings from the original words.

The word *circus* is spelled the same in English and in Latin. The meaning, however, has changed over time. In the days of the Romans, a circus first meant a place where animals and gladiators fought to the death. Later the word *circus* came to mean the event itself. Today, a circus means an event of fun, nonviolent entertainment for children and adults.

Section 3 Summary

Roman Social Classes

Roman society had three social classes: the rich, the poor, and slaves. Most poor Romans were either slaves or jobless. Most of the jobless relied on government help.

The rich often had beautiful homes in the cities. They also had second homes called **villas**. Wealthy Romans were famous for overdoing things.

Most people, though, lived in poorly built, run-down housing. Many lived in tall apartment houses. They had no running water, toilets, or kitchens. Rubbish and human waste was dumped out the window. Most houses were made of wood, so many homes burned down. The worst fire destroyed most of the city in A.D. 64.

Poor citizens needed wheat for bread to survive. Sometimes harvests were bad or grain shipments were late. This caused the poor to riot. To stop the unrest, the emperors gave free grain to the poor. They also provided spectacular shows. These were held in the Colosseum or in arenas called **circuses**. The shows came to be called circuses, too.

Circuses were violent. They had fights between animals, between animals and humans, and between humans. The highlights were the fights between **gladiators**, who fought to the death. Most gladiators were captured slaves. ✓

The Roman Family

Most Romans had strong traditional values. They valued family life. The Roman government encouraged this value and helped families. Upper classes were rewarded for having more children. But there were punishments for unmarried men over 20 and couples with no children.

Key Terms

villa (VIL uh) *n.* a large country estate
circus (SUR kus) *n.* an arena in ancient Rome; the show held there
gladiator (GLAD ee ay tur) *n.* a person in ancient Rome who fought in an arena for the entertainment of the public

Vocabulary Strategy

In Latin, the word *circus* came from a Greek word that meant "circle." What does this tell you about the shape of the arenas the Roman called circuses?

____

____

____

✓ Reading Check

What events took place in a Roman circus?

____

____

____

Target Reading Skill

Underline the words and phrases in the bracketed paragraph that signal the sequence of events.

Mark the Text

✓ Reading Check

What rights did men and women have in ancient Rome?

___

___

___

✓ Reading Check

Who owned slaves in ancient Rome?

___

___

___

Under Roman law, the father had complete power in the home. He owned his wife, children, and slaves. In the early days, he could sell his children as slaves. Later, this power was limited.

How much freedom a woman had depended on her husband's wealth and status. Rich women had a lot of freedom. Women also had a strong influence on their families. The mothers or wives of some emperors gained great political power. ✓

Slavery in Rome

Slavery was common in ancient Rome. Most wealthy families owned slaves. About a third of Italy's people were slaves by 50 B.C. Slaves had almost no rights. Relationships between household slaves and their owners were sometimes friendly. These slaves helped raise children and served as companions. Sometimes they rose to important positions in their owners' homes. ✓

Slaves who worked in a home were treated best. Other kinds of slaves often led short, brutal lives. Slaves on farms sometimes worked chained together and slept chained together. Conditions for slaves in the mines were terrible. Gladiator slaves risked death every time they fought. Roman warships were powered by slaves trained as rowers.

Some slaves were able to save tips or wages and buy their freedom. Slaves with special athletic skills could become famous heroes.

Review Questions

1. Why did the Roman government feed and entertain its people?

___

___

___

2. What kinds of roles and jobs did slaves perform in ancient Rome?

___

___

___

Prepare to Read

Section 4 Christianity and the Roman Empire

Objectives

1. Find out about the rise of Christianity in the Roman Empire.
2. Learn about the spread of Christianity and its effect on the Roman Empire.

Target Reading Skill

Identifying Sequence A sequence is the order in which a series of events occurs. You can keep track of a sequence of events. To do this, list the events in the order in which they happened.

As you read this section, list the events from the rise of Christianity to its spread to Rome. Use a chart like the one below to record the sequence of events.

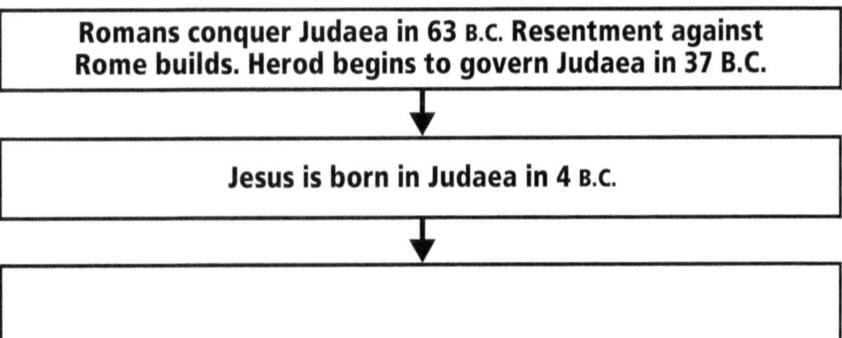

Vocabulary Strategy

Using Word Origins Dozens of English words about Christianity come from Greek or Latin. Some Greek words came into English through Latin. Latin became the language of the Roman Catholic Church. The table below shows a few English words and their Latin and Greek origins. Watch for the English words as you read this section.

English Word	Latin Word	Greek Word
Bible	*biblia*, "book"	*biblos*, "papyrus"
Christ	*Christus*	*christos*, "the anointed"
epistle	*epistola*	*epistole*, "letter"
Messiah	*Messias*	*Messias*, "anointed"

Section 4 Summary

Jesus was the founder of Christianity. In the beginning, most of his followers were poor people and slaves. Over time, the religion spread over the Roman Empire.

The Beginnings of Christianity

Christianity was one of many religions in the Roman Empire. The Romans allowed conquered people some freedom of religion. But they still had to honor Roman gods.

The Romans conquered Judaea in 63 B.C. At first, they let the Jews worship their God. But many Jews did not like foreign rule. Some believed a **messiah** would free them. Opposition to Roman rule grew. As a punishment, the Romans appointed a new ruler of Judaea in 37 B.C. His name was Herod (HEHR ud). Jesus was born during Herod's reign. ✓

Stories about Jesus are found in the New Testament. It is part of the Christian Bible. After Jesus died, his **disciples** told stories about his life and teachings. Some years after his death, four stories of his life were written down as the Gospels.

When Jesus was about 30 years old, he began teaching. Much of what he taught was part of Jewish tradition. He preached that there was only one God. His followers were to love God with all their hearts and their neighbors as themselves. He promised that people who followed his teachings would have everlasting life. His followers believed that he was their messiah.

Jesus' teachings alarmed many people. The Romans feared that he would lead an armed revolt. Jesus was condemned to death and crucified, or put to death by being nailed to a wooden cross. According to the Gospels, Jesus rose from the dead and spoke to his disciples. He told them to spread his teachings.

Key Terms

Jesus (JEE zus) *n.* (c. 4 B.C.–A.D. 29) founder of Christianity; believed by his followers to be the Messiah
messiah (muh SY uh) *n.* a savior in Judaism and Christianity
disciple (dih SY pul) *n.* a follower of a person or a belief

✓ Reading Check

How did the Romans react when Jews opposed Roman rule?

____

____

____

Vocabulary Strategy

The Key Term *disciple* comes from the Latin word *discipulus*, which means "learner." If Jesus' disciples were learners, what does this make Jesus?

____

____

____

Target Reading Skill

What events led to the execution of Jesus?

____

____

____

Christianity Spreads

The Greek word for *messiah* was *christos*. Many educated people of the time spoke Greek. As they accepted Jesus' teachings, they called him Christ. After his death, his followers were called Christians. They spread the new religion from Jerusalem to Rome.

One of Jesus' most faithful disciples was a Jew named Saul. He accepted Christianity and changed his name to Paul after he had a vision in which Jesus spoke to him. After this, he spread Christianity to the cities around the Mediterranean. Paul wrote **epistles** that became a part of the Christian Bible.

Christians would not worship Roman gods. So, many Roman officials saw them as enemies of the empire. When the city burned in A.D. 64, it is thought that the emperor Nero blamed the Christians. Christians, including Paul, were arrested or put to death.

At times over the next 250 years, the Romans punished Christians. Then the Roman Empire began to lose power. The Christians were blamed again. Still, Christianity spread through the empire. Many liked its message of hope for a better life after death.

The emperor Diocletian (dy uh KLEE shuhn) outlawed Christian services. He killed many believers. However, other Romans liked the Christians. They saw them as **martyrs** and heroes. By the A.D. 200s, over 50,000 Romans were Christians. ✓

✓ Reading Check

What did the Romans think of early Christians?

____

____

____

Review Questions

1. What ideas did Jesus teach?

____

____

2. How did Paul's writings effect Christianity?

____

____

Key Terms

epistle (ee PIS ul) *n.* a letter; in the Christian Bible, any of the letters written by disciples to Christian groups
martyr (MAHR tur) *n.* a person who dies for a cause he or she believes in

Prepare to Read

Section 5 The Fall of Rome

Objectives

1. Learn about the causes of the decline of the Roman Empire.
2. Find out how the Roman government came to accept Christianity.
3. Examine the events that marked the defeat of Rome.

Target Reading Skill

Identify Sequence This section is about the decline and fall of the Roman Empire. Use a chart like the one below to follow the sequence of those events. In the "Causes" box, list the events that led to the division of the Roman Empire. In the "Effects" box, list the events that followed the division.

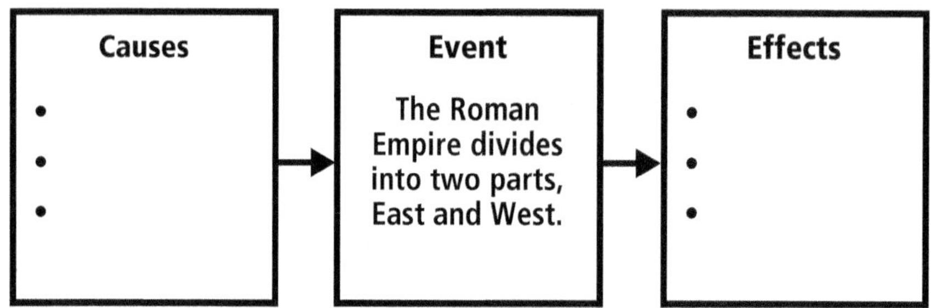

Vocabulary Strategy

Using Word Origins Hundreds of English words come from names of people or places. For example, people who follow the teachings of Jesus are called *Christians*. Christ was the name his followers called him.

The planet Mars is named after the Roman god of war. The ancient city of Constantinople was named after the Roman ruler Constantine. A Vandal was originally a member of a Germanic tribe. Today, the word *vandal* means a person who destroys property. Knowing the history of words can help you to understand and remember new words.

Section 5 Summary

The Decline of the Empire

The emperor Marcus Aurelius was known for his wisdom. After his death, his son Commodus became emperor in A.D. 180. He was a mean ruler. He bribed the army to support him. The decline of the Roman Empire began under Commodus. Other problems also led to Rome's end.

The 29 emperors who followed Commodus were weak and corrupt. They were not politicians but generals who gained power through violence. Many stole money from the government. They used the money to become rich and pay off the soldiers. In the end the senate lost its power.

At one time, the Roman army had been made up of citizen soldiers. Now, it was filled with **mercenaries**. They often switched sides to make more money. Rome's strength had depended on a strong army loyal to the empire. It no longer had one. ✓

The Roman Empire had grown too big to be ruled from one place. Tribes that the Romans had conquered now invaded the empire. Some of the conquered regions broke away. The army spent all its time defending the empire instead of gaining new land. The empire shrank.

When Rome stopped conquering new lands, there were no new sources of wealth. The empire struggled to pay its army. To raise money, taxes were raised. At the same time, many people did not have jobs. Food was scarce, so prices went up. To pay for it, the government produced more money. The new coins had less silver in them. This resulted in **inflation**. Money bought less and less until Roman coins were worth nothing.

Key Terms

mercenary (MUR suh neh ree) *n.* a soldier who serves for pay in a foreign army
inflation (in FLAY shun) *n.* an economic situation in which there is more money of less value

✓ Reading Check

Why did a mercenary army cause problems for the empire?

Target Reading Skill

What is the order of events in the bracketed paragraph that led the value of Roman coins to decline?

The emperor Diocletian tried to save Rome. He split the empire into two parts to make it easier to control. He ruled the wealthier east. A co-emperor ruled the west.

The Romans Accept Christianity

Diocletian retired in A.D. 305. Several generals then fought for power. **Constantine** won. He believed that the Christian God had helped him to win. A year later, he said that all people could worship as they wished. Soon, Christianity was the accepted religion of the Roman Empire.

Constantine made the city of Byzantium (bih ZAN tee um) his capital. He renamed the city Constantinople. The empire's power was now in the east. ✓

The Defeat of Rome

After Constantine's death, invaders from the north swept in. Today, we call them Germanic tribes. The Romans called them barbarians. One tribe, the Visigoths, took Rome in 410. Another tribe, the Vandals, took Rome in 455. The Roman emperor could not stop them.

The last Roman emperor was a 14-year-old called Romulus Augustulus. In 476, a German general took power and sent the boy to work on a farm. After him, no emperor ruled the western part of the empire. But, the eastern part of the empire stayed strong for 1,000 years. It became the Byzantine Empire. ✓

✓ Reading Check

What city became the new capital of the Roman Empire?

____

____

____

Vocabulary Strategy

Originally, a Vandal was a member of a Germanic tribe. Now a vandal is a person who destroys property. How do you think the word *vandal* got this meaning?

____

____

____

✓ Reading Check

Who was Romulus Augustulus, and what was his fate?

____

____

____

Review Questions

1. List at least five problems that led to the decline of the Roman Empire.

____

____

2. What did Constantine do to show that he accepted Christianity?

____

____

Key Term

Constantine (KAHN stuhn teen) *n.* (c. A.D. 286–337) emperor of Rome from A.D. 312 to 337; encouraged the spread of Christianity

Chapter 7 Assessment

1. In the Roman Republic, what happened if the two consuls disagreed in an emergency?
   A. A dictator was appointed.
   B. A third consul was appointed.
   C. The senate made the final decision.
   D. A new government was elected.

2. Many Romans visited Greece to study
   A. Greek art and architecture.
   B. ideas about government.
   C. both a and b
   D. none of the above

3. Which of the following was NOT a Roman social class?
   A. patricians
   B. plebeians
   C. slaves
   D. gladiators

4. The letters written by the disciple Paul, called epistles, became part of
   A. the Gospels.
   B. the Christian Bible.
   C. Hadrian's laws.
   D. the Jewish Torah.

5. The Roman emperor who allowed Christianity in Rome was
   A. Marcus Aurelius.
   B. Commodus.
   C. Constantine.
   D. Romulus Augustulus.

Short Answer Question

How did the lives of the rich and poor differ in ancient Rome?

____

____

____

____

____